Miss Emma Lehman

The Class of 1904

THOMAS WOLFE AT WASHINGTON SQUARE

THOMAS WOLFE

AT

WASHINGTON SQUARE

BY

THOMAS CLARK POLLOCK

AND OSCAR CARGILL

New York University Press

WASHINGTON SQUARE · NEW YORK

1954

FIRST PRINTING, JANUARY 1954
SECOND PRINTING, JULY 1954

TO THE MEMORY OF

Robert Bruce Dow & John Skally Terry

COLLEAGUES AND FRIENDS OF

THOMAS WOLFE

PREFACE

OUR PURPOSE in publishing this book is twofold: to place in the hands of those interested as careful an account as we have been able to put together of the connection of Thomas Clayton Wolfe with the Washington Square College of New York University and of his life and development during that period; and, with our royalties from the sale of this volume and its companion, to create a prize or scholarship in Wolfe's name to aid some student like "Abe Jones" in his unapplauded quest for an education.

We derive this purpose from Professor Homer Andrew Watt, late chairman of the Department of English of the College, who was Wolfe's employer, immediate superior, and always a timely friend. Dr. Watt conceived the idea for the book shortly after Tom's death, but, though he was better equipped than anyone else to write and edit it, the harassments that fell to his post during the depression, the Second World War, and the postwar expansion, followed by a subtle and debilitating illness which he faced with a courage that took all his strength, kept him from ever drafting more than eleven pages of an introductory essay, occupied largely by full quotation from the first exchange of letters between Tom and himself.

When we picked up the task, we had a very clear sense of our inadequacy for it. But the obligation was a sacred one: Dr. Watt had summoned Mr. Pollock to his bedside in the French Hospital late in his final illness, had secured a pledge for the completion of the book, and had designated Mr. Cargill to assist him. We were aware that there were living many people who could complete such an assignment out of an intimacy which we never enjoyed and who would instantly detect our errors and shortcomings. We still expect these to be exposed, but we are, perhaps, entitled to hope that the strictures will be laid with an understanding charity.

Originally we were agreed that Mr. Pollock would do the leading essay, since Mr. Cargill feared that his slight acquaintance with Tom Wolfe would be more of a handicap than an aid in achieving any sort of factualism. But the responsibilities of the deanship and other duties which became the lot of Mr. Pollock prevented him from carrying out this plan. Hence Mr. Cargill has written the leading essay and takes full responsibility for its omissions and shortcomings, whatever they are. While working on the book we tried to reach as many former students and colleagues of Wolfe as possible for information about him in this period of his life; the interest of our replies suggested making a section of Memorabilia out of some of them that we had not employed almost in their entirety in the leading essay. It should be pointed out, however, that none of the writers of pieces included in the Memorabilia section had the advantage of seeing what the others had written about Wolfe. To the whole, a Bibliography has been added as a useful critical tool.

Our original plan had been to publish both *The Correspondence of Thomas Wolfe and Homer Andrew Watt* and *Thomas Wolfe at Washington Square* in one volume, but a number of practical considerations in relation to permissions made the present form of publication the only practicable one.

Though we have used Wolfe's fiction to illuminate our narrative, we trust we have not used it indiscriminately, without other sustaining evidence — evidence not always possible to present. Especially would we caution the reader against assuming that, when Wolfe drew a portrait from life, no fictional elements were added to the character of the person used as a model. We do not feel responsible for the attribution of traits to characters in Wolfe's fiction that lie beyond the province of our own book, and it should be noted that we repudiate many of the ascriptions that come within that province.

We have been abundantly aided, and here we gratefully acknowledge our indebtedness to the following persons:

Miss Jean B. Barr, Waldo Buckham, Miss Jean Casper, Harry A. Charipper, Harry Woodburn Chase, Robert B. Dow, A. Gerald Doyle, Theodore G. Ehrsam, Vardis Fisher, Boris Gamzue, Mrs. Helen H. Gude, David D. Henry, William A. Jackson, Miss Kathleen M. Jones, Abraham I. Katsh, Richard S. Kennedy, LeRoy E. Kimball, Bernard W. Kofsky, Miss Charlotte Kohler, Russell Krauss, George W. McCoy, Bruce McCullough, James L. Mandel, Henry Allen Moe, James B. Munn, Miss Elizabeth Nowell, Joseph H. Park, Albert S. Pegues, Desmond Powell, John R. Schoemer, Jr., Miss Catherine Ruth Smith, John Skally Terry, James Thurber, William Tindall, Miss Peggy Tower, Henry T. Volkening, William W. Watt, Miss Jean N. Weston, John Hall Wheelock, and Arthur Zeiger. Mr. and Mrs. George Horstein jointly aided us.

To Miss Nowell and Mr. Kennedy and to the late John Skally Terry we owe a special debt of gratitude for their reading of the leading essay and the suggestions they have offered us out of their long study and research in the career of Thomas Wolfe.

Finally we wish to thank the legal firms of Townley, Updike & Carter and Gerdes & Montgomery for valuable advice in the course of this undertaking.

THOMAS CLARK POLLOCK
OSCAR CARGILL

September 3, 1953

TABLE OF CONTENTS

ACKNOWLEDGMENTS

We wish to acknowledge the privilege of using the following materials in copyright in this book:

The Arizona Quarterly and Desmond Powell for the passage from "Of Thomas Wolfe."

The Atlantic Monthly and Donald B. Snyder, publisher, for the passages from Thomas Wolfe's "Writing Is My Life."

Theodore G. Ehrsam for the passage from "I Knew Thomas Wolfe" in *Fact Digest.*

Harper & Brothers for the passages from Thomas Wolfe's *The Web and the Rock.*

Harvard Library Bulletin for the passages from Maxwell Perkins' essay, "Thomas Wolfe."

Charles Scribner's Sons for the passages from Thomas Wolfe's *Of Time and the River* and from *Thomas Wolfe's Letters to His Mother,* edited by John Skally Terry.

Tomorrow and Eileen J. Garrett, publisher, and Vardis Fisher for the essay "My Experiences with Thomas Wolfe."

The Virginia Quarterly Review and Henry T. Volkening for the essay "Tom Wolfe: Penance No More."

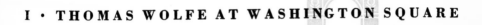

I · THOMAS WOLFE AT WASHINGTON SQUARE

THOMAS WOLFE

AT WASHINGTON SQUARE

> He took those . . . swarming classes and looted his life
> clean for them: he bent over them, prayed, sweated, and
> exhorted like a prophet, a poet, and a priest — he poured
> upon them the whole deposit of his living, feeling, read-
> ing, the whole store of poetry, passion, and belief . . . .
>
> —*Of Time and the River*

THOMAS WOLFE lived, created, and died without reaching Thackeray's prescriptive age for a novelist. Focal in that compacted, turbulent career was not his Asheville boyhood, his Chapel Hill or Cambridge student days, his harvest years of fame in Europe or America, but those experience-drenched hours he passed in New York City between 1924 and 1930 when he sustained himself as a teacher in the Washington Square College of New York University. At the time of his graduation from the University of North Carolina in June 1920, a teaching position in English had been offered him by Colonel Robert Bingham, headmaster of the Bingham School, a military academy in Asheville, on the recommendation of Tom's teachers at the university.[1] Eager to go on to Harvard to study playwrighting under Professor George Pierce Baker in the already famous 47 Workshop[2] and assured of his mother's financial aid after his father, a stonecutter in Asheville who had seen him through his

Notes may be found on pages 67-84.

studies at North Carolina, had furiously declined to carry him further, Wolfe decided against accepting Colonel Bingham's offer, though it meant that he might have remained in Asheville during his father's illness.[3] A letter in September from Cambridge to his mother, defensive in character, shows that he then regarded teaching as stultifying and sure to blight his genius. At Harvard he had been admitted to English 47, the Workshop course, by special dispensation since he had not conformed to the requirement of submitting a play a year in advance: his work under Frederick H. Koch, however, was a sufficient recommendation to Baker.[4] He had also undertaken a program leading to the M.A. degree and was to do so well in it during the coming year that it was again suggested to him that he teach, an idea that he immediately rejected.[5]

He was very much alone in his first year at Harvard and devoted the bulk of it to reading "prodigiously" in the Widener Library, which, he noted expansively, "has crumbled under my savage attack, ten, twelve, fifteen books a day are nothing."[6] Nevertheless he had a one-act play, "The Mountains," tried out in the Workshop in January.[7] In the spring he began work on a long play, which he first called "The Heirs" or "The Wasters," then "The House," and finally *Mannerhouse*.[8] In the spring also he vowed to turn "The Mountains" into "a great play, a long play . . . someday,"[9] but it would not appear that he did anything toward this in the academic year 1920-1921. By June he had unconsciously done more to prepare himself for teaching than he had done consciously to discipline himself for playwrighting.

He may or may not have made efforts during the summer of 1921 to find part-time employment while continuing to take courses in the Harvard summer school, but the country was caught in a minor depression and no work was available. "Within a half course" of his master's degree because of his summer courses[10] but with a "condition" in French still to remove, he began a campaign to get his mother to sustain him for another year in Cambridge, first rehearsing his accomplishment in the intolerable heat ("We have nothing

4

at home to compare with it."), then a whole calendar of illnesses and afflictions, and finally charging her with indifference: "You would not be intentionally guilty of cruelty to me but unintentionally you have been. Uncle Henry says it is a family trait to forget once out of sight — but how in God's name can I believe you would forget me in a year's time." To this was added a veiled, adolescent threat: "You didn't want me at home, you said nothing about my returning and I shall see that your desires and those of the family are satisfied."[11] However hard a head and heart the marble man's wife possessed, neither was sturdy enough to resist this variety of assault, and Wolfe's tactics, supplemented by increasingly glowing accounts of his prospects in the theater, won him another year at Harvard. During the year he completed the requirements for the M.A. degree, which was awarded him in June. His chief effort in the Workshop seems to have been to expand "The Mountains" into a full-length play.[12] Wolfe was by now better known to his Workshop classmates, and his reiterated belief in his destiny began to be both mildly amusing and annoying to them. His neglect of his person, his shabby attire, his extraordinary physique, and his habits must have produced both sly and open ridicule, and when Baker warmed to him and, after reading the prologue of "The Mountains" to the class in the spring of 1922, pronounced it "the best prolog ever written here,"[13] envy edged the ridicule with malice. It became a situation in which the advocate of folk plays stood alone against the aesthetes, and Wolfe possibly began then to deride the "artist myth" later ridiculed in his notebook.[14] In May 1922 the annual musical show, "The 47 Varieties," burlesqued "The Mountains" in raucous verses.[15] It was not shattered belief in his genius, however, that led Wolfe to register with the Harvard Appointment Office, whose sole function was to find teaching jobs for Harvard men, for he specified that, if he could not be placed in a position near Cambridge, "I will be sent to New York or some large centre where I can keep in touch with the theatre."[16] He knew his mother would not support him for another year at Harvard. Teaching could be a "tide-me-over" if it did not cut him off from his writing career.

The Appointment Office in June 1922 recommended Wolfe for a position at Northwestern University in Chicago, but he abandoned all thought of teaching when he learned that his father was dying, and he hurriedly left for Asheville to be there at the end. He did not make it, but from his voluble relatives he got enough details to fashion the lurid account of his father's death, or that of "W. O. Gant," that appears in *Of Time and the River*.[17] On August 22, 1922, he notified the Appointment Office that he was returning to Harvard for another year, and he did so, registering for a single course, English 47a, the advanced course in the Workshop. Just how he managed his third year at Harvard is not known. Wolfe's father left each child about $5,000, but Tom is supposed to have pledged his whole inheritance against his expenditures at the University of North Carolina and at Harvard.[18] But this may not have been the case, or he may by personal appeal have succeeded in getting his mother to stake him further. He had, when he returned to the Workshop, parts of no less than six plays; Professor Baker got him, however, to concentrate on one. Based on material picked up in Asheville, it was first called "Niggertown" and dealt with the scheme of white promoters in a Southern city to evict Negro tenants from a slum area in order to develop a white residential section there. Wolfe continued to devour books and worked hard on this play the whole year: by December 1 he had the prologue and first act done; he finished another scene during the Christmas holidays; and read the whole play, now called "Welcome to Our City," to the class on January 16.[19] By March, Professor Baker had determined to give it Workshop production and had set May 15 as the date of its première. Three months were devoted to condensation and revision, but when the play was finally presented at the Agassiz Theatre it was one of the longest and most ambitious undertaken by the Workshop: the performance ran from 8:00 P.M. to midnight, and there were ten scenes, seven changes of setting, and thirty-one speaking parts.[20] Wolfe hoped that Richard Herndon, the New York producer who gave an annual prize of $500 for the best Workshop play, might be induced to purchase "Welcome to Our City," but Herndon did not embrace his opportunity.[21] Professor Baker undertook to interest the Theatre Guild in the play and was able to secure a reading. It was indicated to Wolfe, however, that he must cut "Welcome to Our City" so that it could be presented in two hours and a half — standard Broadway production time — if he wanted an acceptance.[22]

Baker, in the meantime, had urged Wolfe to go up to his summer home in New Hampshire in June to finish writing his "new" play, probably *Mannerhouse*.[23] Wolfe declined the invitation because he felt that he needed to be near the Widener Library. He remained in Cambridge all summer, except for two three-day excursions, but he frittered away his time and did not submit his revised manuscript to the Theatre Guild until early September.[24] He then asked Professor Baker to write his mother, evidently in support of a petition for financial aid to enable him to live in Cambridge. "At the present time I could stand the loss of anything except what faith you have in me," he told Julia Elizabeth Wolfe. Tom went to New York and stayed in the city or its vicinity, except for a trip to Asheville in October, from the time he submitted the play until the Christmas holidays of 1923 — after the play had been rejected by the Theatre Guild.[25] In turning down "Welcome to Our City," Courtenay Lemon, reader for the Guild, and Lawrence Langner, one of its directors, treated Wolfe with the greatest consideration. Lemon intimated that the handling of the race issue was not wholly satisfactory, and both men insisted that the play was still too long. Neither, however, saw any reason why it could not be revised to their satisfaction.[26] Kennedy believes that the play was fundamentally weak because Wolfe had not resolved the conflict in his own mind on his attitude toward the Negro. Because of this, the drawing of his principals, Rutledge the white leader, and Johnson the black, is not good.[27] Rejection left Wolfe purposeless until his money was nearly gone.

Among Wolfe's friends in New York City at this time were two who proved helpful to him — George Wallace and Robert Dow. Wallace, formerly a successful advertising man in Detroit, was now taking writing courses at Columbia and knocking around the city nights with Wolfe. Though all of forty years of age, he had given up his job the previous year to do graduate work at Harvard and to study English composition under Dean Briggs. He wished to become a creative writer. He had not then sufficient educational background to gain admission to the Workshop, but he reverenced those who did, especially Tom Wolfe, whose companion he became in Cambridge. "A generous, kindly, enthusiastic man, somewhat pathetic in his purpose to convert his life," he has been described as "a most warming friend to Wolfe." Robert Dow, whose acerb speech concealed a tremendous fund of good nature, was a New Hampshire man who held a Dartmouth degree. He, too, had done graduate work at Harvard, where, through Wallace, he had met Tom on a couple of occasions and had attended the performance of "Welcome to Our City." In the autumn of 1923 he had been appointed Instructor in English at University College, in New York University, the older of the two liberal arts colleges of that institution, located on "the Heights" opposite the Palisades and some thirteen miles from Washington Square where Tom eventually was to teach. He had joined Wallace and Wolfe on some of their prowls, becoming better acquainted with the latter and once doing a peripatetic stint of thirty-four blocks with him. Friendship led Wolfe to confide his utter lack of prospects and to inquire of Dow if he might not secure something at New York University. Dow, who had not been aware that Tom had taken any courses outside the Workshop, learned from Wallace for the first time that Wolfe had achieved an M.A. in literature and encouraged him to apply for appointment,[28] indicating there might be an opening at "the Heights." Tom excitedly wrote his mother about this opportunity and reported his intention to run up to Cambridge to get the Appointment Office to send his credentials to New York University.[29]

Since he could have written the Appointment Office to forward his papers, Wolfe's real purpose in returning to Cambridge was probably to consult Professor Baker about the advisability of teaching until he could establish himself as a playwright. He anticipated that Baker would veto the idea but he was prepared to argue for it himself.

> . . . Baker will raise h--l when he hears of my decision to teach, but as I have not yet learned the secret of living exclusively on wind and water — there's no way out. My money's almost gone — I have fifteen or twenty dollars left — enough to get me to Boston or New Hampshire and the Univ. owes me a little more. I am going to try to borrow two or three hundred dollars in Boston, to buy clothing and tide me over until I get to work. If I fail in this I may have to ask you for an advance.[30]

Baker, in Tom's words, "hit the ceiling over the teaching proposition and said that it would never do" — it would allow him no chance for writing and might damage his talent. He advised Tom not to waste time as he had in the last four months but to settle down and write. Tom recounted to his mother how he had told Baker that he could not ask her for more aid, but he sighed for "some benevolent old gentleman, with more money than brains to finance me; or if I could go in debt even, I think I would take the chance."[31] He indicated his intention to make an approach to New York University despite Baker's opposition and asked her to advise him at once on what he should do. He called her attention casually in closing to the fact that Oliver M. Sayler had mentioned his play in his recent book, *Our American Theatre*.[32] Although his letter is, despite its disclaimer, one of solicitation, he could not have expected too much from it. From *Of Time and the River* it seems likely that he believed that others were encouraging Mrs. Wolfe to be more obdurate than she might have been alone,[33] but it may be that this interference was wholly imagined, or fictional. Nevertheless he waited nearly a week before he addressed a letter to Homer Andrew Watt, chairman of the Department of English of Washington Square College of New York University, though Dow, through Wallace, urged immediacy.[34]

In writing Dr. Watt on January 10, 1924, Wolfe chose simplicity and candor — traits, though he could not have known this, most appealing to the person whom he addressed and possessed by the latter in a marked degree. Homer Andrew Watt, a native of Wilkes-Barre, Pennsylvania, and one of a pair of identical twins, was of Scotch-English descent, with the Scotch blood predominating. He was a man of immense energy, resourcefulness, and vision. Exploited (as he felt) by the University of Wisconsin, where he took his doctorate in 1909 and where he was kept as an instructor without promotion for seven years, though much of the drudgery of the administration of the required composition course fell upon him, he was against the exploitation of young instructors, but this warm impulse was checked by lack of means and a thrifty desire to do the best with what he had. He was a religious man in the very formal sense, occupying important posts in suburban Presbyterian and Congregational churches in the different towns in New Jersey in which he resided, but his Calvinism was tempered in the direction of expecting more than ordinary fallibility in fallible man and of accommodating that expectation with more than ordinary charity. No man in his employ ever fell ill or erred without discovering how much tenderness lay behind the pale blue eyes, firm lips, and salient lower jaw. The sinner, to be sure, could expect some plain speaking, but a sentence was more common than a sermon. Let an outsider assail one of his staff, however, and Dr. Watt was up in arms. It was surprising that a man who had so strong a sense of hierarchy would stand up against deans and chancellors for a two-penny instructor lately come out of Bohemia or Harvard whose folly or scoundrelism was apparent to everybody but his chairman. Thus some arrant rascals had a longer term in his department than either their behavior or talents warranted.

Yet fluidity was more characteristic of the department in which Wolfe hoped to teach, and over which Dr. Watt presided, than was permanence. New York University was expanding very rapidly in response to population growth in the metropolis, which had not the four great free colleges, with their branches, that it has today. A private school, subsisting chiefly on student fees, New York University had expanded from 4,300 students in 1912 to 16,000 in 1923, the year before Wolfe began his teaching there; it was to have an enrollment of over 30,000 in 1931, the year after Wolfe left, and to reach over 65,000 before 1950.[35] Between 1916 when Dr. Watt joined the faculty as an assistant professor and 1924 when Wolfe applied for appointment, the liberal arts college on the east side of Washington Square was practically re-created. This had been the original site of University College, but in the early nineties Chancellor Henry Mitchell MacCracken had conceived that what the metropolis desired was a campus college and he had transferred University College uptown — in fact, all but out of town — to a very beautiful but inaccessible location on Fordham Heights, renamed University Heights, in the Bronx. The University had retained ownership, however, of the original site on Washington Square, but the old Gothic building that once housed the college had been torn down and a new ten-story building had been erected by the University in its place. An understanding had been reached with the American Book Company that it would lease all but the top two stories, which were reserved to house the Graduate School and the Schools of Law and Pedagogy.[36] Because it had been decided, in 1904, that degrees in pedagogy would be given only to those students who held the baccalaureate degree, a Collegiate Division, so-called, had been re-established at the Square, primarily for the benefit of normal-school students who could not attend the school at the Heights. The slow but steady growth of the Collegiate Division led Chancellor Elmer Ellsworth Brown, who had succeeded Dr. MacCracken, to recommend to the Council of the University, over the opposition of University College and the former Chancellor, the transformation of this division into Washington Square College, and this was formally done on January 1, 1914. The new college had no dean until 1917 and no resident faculty until 1918. Chancellor Brown acted as dean until John R. Turner was appointed in 1917, and the teaching was done by staff members of the other schools.[37] Thus Dr. Watt was appointed in the Department of English at University College, though from the start it was understood that part of his work would be at the Square, and shortly he was transferred there as one of the first members of the resident faculty.

Development of Washington Square College would have proceeded faster had it not been for World War I and the short business recession immediately following it. Not only were Columbia College, Barnard, Hunter, and the City College inadequate to meet the tremendous demand for higher education that developed in the second decade of the twentieth century but they were not so advantageously located as was the school at this center. East and south of Washington Square was the densest population in New York; product of an unrestricted immigration prior to 1910, it had not been urged out of the area by anything comparable to the force that brought it there, with the result that it settled in and began its own rehabilitation. Every block witnessed the start of scores of business successes, particularly during the booming twenties, and parents who had been denied an education themselves, prizing it more highly than any group in American history has prized education, save possibly the founders of New England, urged their children into the "new" college that was developing at Washington Square. The ambitious sons and daughters of the less fortunate emulated their friends by going to college, too, but they had to earn their way by part-time employment when they were not in school. With this core to give it substance and good fortune in the character of some of the faculty, brought together as much by chance as design, the College began to attract students beyond its immediate locale. Then the great advantage of its site became still more apparent. Here all the subway lines then existing — the Broadway B.M.T., the Seventh Avenue I.R.T., and the Lexington Avenue lines — converged within a block or two of each other. Here the screeching Sixth Avenue Elevated, after coming up West Broadway to Bleecker and turning west across the bottom of the Square to the Avenue, all but caught the University in a loop. And here the route of the Fifth Avenue bus lines terminated and at Ninth Street the Hudson-Manhattan tubes disgorged students from Jersey City and beyond. If he thought a playing field and ivy unessential, a city planner could not have located a university more perfectly. By 1922 the American Book Company had been forced out of all but the two lower floors of the Main Building and was preparing to depart completely, and the College had spilled over into the adjacent Brown Building, scene of the terrible Triangle fire of March 25, 1911.[38] The University leased this building, but eventually it became University property through the gift of Mr. and Mrs. Frederick Brown.[39]

Who could be sure in the early twenties that this influx of students would last? Or, more important, what in any given year the dimensions of the student body would be? Uncertainty dictated a policy of improvisation and fluidity — in the first stages of this growth instructors had to be hired on a yearly or even a half-yearly basis. To a young man with his doctorate, ambitious to establish himself in his profession, Washington Square College then offered too little certainty to be attractive. But the colleges in New York City in the twenties had a great attraction for two types of young people: the person who had a master's degree[40] and wished to push on to the doctorate and who had no other way to finance himself but to teach and the person who had a literary career in view and wished, not only means to support himself, but companionship with persons of like aims and tastes. Because of its proximity to Greenwich Village, then famous for its bookshops, studios, little magazines, theater, literary and artistic groups, inexpensive restaurants, and cheap lodgings (fifteen dollars a month would get a cold-water flat and several instructors might combine to rent a furnished house for sixty or seventy), Washington Square College had an appeal

13

beyond Columbia, Barnard, Hunter, or City College, though all were actually flooded with applicants. To choose teachers of ability and good character from this horde to whom the tutelage of the young might safely be entrusted required unusual perceptiveness, intuition, and luck, since the incompetent and the unreliable frequently came with the highest recommendations. The turnover of instructors was great, for many glaringly demonstrated their incompetence in one way or another; others, discouraged in the pursuit of the doctorate or literary fame, struck their tents and departed; still others fell into dissipation or ill-health and had to give up, while a few, achieving success, found its continuance or final realization elsewhere. That he managed to staff his department successfully under the unusual circumstances in which he labored and that he steadily improved the quality of that department were the highest achievements of Dr. Watt's career, though he managed at the same time to accumulate a fortune and a national reputation as a textbook maker.[41]

Wolfe placed himself in the second category of applicants by declaring that he had no experience as a teacher, that his real interest was the drama, and that he hoped someday to write successfully for the theater and do nothing else. He mentioned the startling effect that his unusual stature might have ("my height is four or five inches over six feet"), and he pledged his best effort if appointed.[42] We are fortunate in knowing how Wolfe's application affected its recipient since Dr. Watt had started to set down his recollections of the novelist just before his death:

> Certain elements in his letter struck me at once. It was direct, it was frank, it was honest. This Thomas Wolfe — whoever he was — did not try to conceal his inexperience as a teacher. He did not even pretend that he wanted to make teaching a lifelong profession but asserted almost bluntly that his chief goal was to write successful plays. He showed a penetrating awareness that if he were to join a college department of English his personal appearance might very "justly enter into any estimates" of his qualifications. His own consciousness

14

of his unusual stature I came to know later as a very sensitive point with him.

I was pleased by his promise at the end of his letter that, if appointed, he would "give the most faithful and efficient service" of which he was capable. Here the applicant did not "protest too much," and his assertion was simple and rang true. When Tom Wolfe finally left the department just six years after he made this promise, I could agree with him that not once had he failed to carry out his initial pledge.[43]

Only one statement in Wolfe's letter of application was perhaps challengeable: "my play is at present in the hands of a producer in New York. . . ." Though he had written his mother on January 4, 1924, that he might "try to shorten my play during the few weeks of grace yet left to me, as the man on the Theatre Guild desires,"[44] there is no positive evidence that he did this, and the statement that a producer had it is probably one of good enough intention rather than actual accomplishment.

In the same mail that brought to Professor Watt the letter of application there came the following "Confidential Statement" about Wolfe from the Harvard Appointment Office:[45]

HARVARD UNIVERSITY

CAMBRIDGE MASS

Harvard Appointment Office
Harvard University
Cambridge, Mass.

information relating to
THOMAS CLAYTON WOLFE

[June 1922]

Revised
January 1924

DEGREES: A.B. University of North Carolina 1920; A.M. Harvard University, 1922.

DISTINCTIONS RECEIVED: Worth Prize in Philosophy (North Carolina) 1919.

COURSE OF STUDY AT HARVARD: English, German, Comparative Literature.

EXPERIENCE IN TEACHING:

REMARKS: Age 23. Height 6 ft. 3½". Weight 182. Presbyterian. Reads French and German fairly well; Interested in baseball and tennis; Has written some two act plays; Member of Freshman Debating Club (North Carolina) also of Carolina Playmakers; Member 47 Workshop (Harvard). also of Satyrs, dramatic; the Golden Fleece (North Carolina).
1918, in the Flying Field, Hampton, (Va.) as Time Checker; also Material Checker for U. S. Government, Newport News (Va.). 1922-23, returned to Harvard and studied in the 47 Workshop. His play, "Welcome to Our City" was produced at the Workshop in May 1923. Mention of this play may be found in Oliver Sayler's recent book on The American Theatre.

ADDRESS: Permanent: 48 Spruce Street, Asheville, N. C.
[67 Hammond Street,
Cambridge, Mass.]
Present: 10 Trowbridge Street, Cambridge, Mass.

[Page 2]

Confidential Information relating to
THOMAS CLAYTON WOLFE

Harvard Appointment Office,   June 1922
11 University Hall,
Cambridge, Mass.

Professor J. L. Lowes, Harvard University, writes 1922:
"A student of very distinct ability who can bury himself in a subject and can come out with fresh and interesting results. His intelligence is keen and alert, and with a little more discipline will be, I think, an instrument of unusual effectiveness."

Professor G. P. Baker, ibid. writes 1922:
"One of the promising students in English 47A, the advanced course in playwriting. Whether he will be a successful playwright some day depends, I think, entirely on himself. He is intelligent, ambitious and well-equipped. I much want him to return for special work another year."

Professor H. H. Williams, Univ. North Carolina, writes 1922:
(Dept. Philosophy)
"I consider Thomas C. Wolfe one of six remarkable students in my thirty years experience here."

Professor F. H. Koch, Professor of Dramatic Literature, ibid. writes 1922:
"I am glad of an opportunity to speak for Mr. Thomas Clayton Wolfe. He was a student in my courses in dramatic literature and composition for two

years — a young man of brilliant mind and rare literary talent. He is possessed of unbounded energy and enthusiasm — is a hard worker, a man of sterling character, and a born leader of men."

Dean Greenlaw, ibid, writes 1922:

"I have an extremely high regard for Mr. Wolfe, both as a student and as a man. He is an exceedingly able writer, a hard worker, and a man of interesting personality."

Professor Watt had few applicants in 1924 who offered any better references than did Tom Wolfe: Baker and Koch were the best men teaching dramatic technique in the country and have not since been surpassed; John Livingston Lowes and Edwin Greenlaw must be ranked among the best English scholars that America has produced — the former famous for his work on Chaucer and Coleridge, the latter for his Spenser studies. If Dr. Watt were not impressed by Wolfe's endorsers and what they said about him, he surely was by the fact that Wolfe avowed himself to be a "Presbyterian." One or two different small points in these papers interest the more recent student of Thomas Wolfe. Here his height is stated as six feet, three and one-half inches and his weight as 182 pounds, whereas in his letter of application he says "my height is four or five inches over six feet" and, in September 1920, his weight had been "over 200 pounds."[46] This raises the interesting question of just how big Tom Wolfe was. Describing himself elsewhere, he calls himself "a queer looking person, some six and a half feet high,"[47] while John Terry, his intimate friend, speaks of the long cot Tom owned as big enough "to accommodate his great six feet, seven inches."[48] Another intimate friend, Julian R. Meade, however, was content to make him "6-foot, 4"[49]; but Homer Bigart, seven months later after an interview, thoughtfully added an inch.[50] "Gulliver," Tom Wolfe's famous, self-conscious story on the disadvantages of unusual height, speaks of "the strangest and most lonely world there is"—"the world of six feet six."[51] He is remembered by Professor Howard Dunbar, who is himself six feet four, as much bigger than he; the author of this essay, whose clearest image of Wolfe is with arms fully extended in extravagant gesture, simply has no accurate idea of his size but remembers him as enormous, an impression he concedes emphasized also by the length of Wolfe's hair and the ill fit of his garments and underscored by the amount of food he could put away which no ordinary mortal could accommodate. Unlike most big men, he was not phlegmatic; manifestly excitable, frequently perspiring, with wilted collar, he gave such an impression of life as to increase one's sense of his bulk. He may not have been six feet six or seven, but if his corpse were exhumed and measured, and it did not match these proportions, no one of his contemporaries who knew him would give the report the slightest credence. It may be that he minimized his height at the Harvard Appointment Office for fear that it would be a handicap to him in getting a job.

Considering the fact that he was not to be outstandingly popular at New York University, it may be puzzling to find Koch recommending him as "a born leader of men." This was not an error in judgment on Koch's part, who was surely thinking of Wolfe's undergraduate career at North Carolina, where he won all sorts of student honors — he was a member of the Freshman Debating Club, the Dialectic Literary Society, Pi Kappa Phi, the Odd Number Chapter of Sigma Upsilon, the Amphoterothen Club, the cabinet of the Y.M.C.A., the Student Council, and the Carolina Playmakers, and he was editor, after occupying lesser posts, of the student paper *Tar Heel* and of the literary periodical, the Carolina *Magazine*.[52] A "joiner" and a campus politician, Tom Wolfe may well have seemed to Koch "a born leader of men."

Three days after Watt received Wolfe's application and papers, he wrote to offer him an instructorship in English in Washington Square College of New York University for the two terms "from February 6 to September 1 or thereabouts, at a salary of $1800 for the full period."[53] He went on to explain that New York City high schools graduated large classes about February 1 and that it was the practice of the College to set up freshman classes to run between that date and the beginning of the regular fall term, so that freshmen, entering in February, could be full-scale sophomores by fall, could join those who had become sophomores the previous June, and thereafter could conform to the regular September to June pattern for college work. Wolfe would receive his pay in eight installments (it happened, however, that this very year the College shifted to a scheme of monthly payments for the February-September group so that he was actually paid like members of the regular September-June staff[54]). Watt told him that he was hiring eight new men for the coming session and intimated that Wolfe should find some congenial spirits among them since there were other would-be creative artists in the lot. On the regular staff, Watt thought that Wolfe would find a kindred spirit in Bruce Carpenter, another 47 Workshop man who was then trying for Broadway production of a play.[55] Watt closed his letter by promising Wolfe that he would not have more than three sections or ninety students to teach, nor more than eight to ten hours of classroom work, and by asking him to report the week before school began. Wolfe wired on January 21 his acceptance of the terms of the instructorship and promised to report on February 1.[56]

Wolfe arrived on Friday, February 1, as he had promised, and met Dr. Watt and other members of the staff on that day.[57] It was Dr. Watt's practice to hold a staff meeting, especially for the benefit of the new men, before a term began, and he may have held one on this day or the following Saturday. If there were such a meeting, Wolfe nowhere reports it. He did, however, like his new associates. At the moment he was chiefly concerned with learning how much time he would have for himself. Some one misled him into believing that he could "easily complete" his work "in and out of class, with three hours a day."[58] With the program assigned him — three courses in Composition — he would have to spend much more time than this in theme reading alone, since four themes an hour is a good average for an experienced teacher. In his three sections, two in Elementary Composition (English 1-2) for students in the general college course, meeting Tuesday, Thursday, and Saturday from

9:00 to 10:00 and 11:00 to 12:00 in the morning, and one in Elementary Composition (English 3-4) for preprofessional students,
meeting Tuesday and Thursday from 4:00 to 5:00 P.M., Wolfe had
104 students[59]— a tremendous load involving about twenty-six
hours a week of theme reading. He had eight class hours but only
two preparations since he repeated one subject. Nevertheless he
could easily spend three or four hours for each hour of classroom
work or about twenty hours a week on preparation. Unless he cut
corners he had a 54-hour week in prospect to fulfill his obligation
to the College, and much less time than he anticipated for writing.
It is a common delusion that, since they have very few class hours
a week, college teachers have many hours for their own enterprises.
Some readers may conclude that Wolfe, who had lived in college
communities for seven years, was singularly unobservant that he
did not know the contrary to be true, but in this instance he had to
rid himself of a general assumption before he could see — which is
harder than seeing alone. He was to pay for it.

When he came to New York, he took a room in the Hotel Albert
on University Place between Eleventh and Twelfth streets, four
blocks directly north of the Main Building of New York University.
He had resided in this hotel some part of the previous idle summer
and fall, and it was natural, since he was not very demanding about
his lodgings, that he should return to it. After some debate with
himself, he decided to remain at the Albert for the year, where he
was assigned Room 2220, which he had for the modest sum of twelve
dollars a week.[60] As the Hotel Leopold, he has hit it off with more
than usual accuracy in *Of Time and the River*:

> The Leopold, although one of the city's smaller hotels, was not a
> single building, but a congeries of buildings, which covered an entire
> block. The central, and main building of the system, was a structure
> of twelve stories, of that anomalous stone and brick construction
> which seems to have enjoyed a vogue in the early nineteen hundreds.
> To the left was a building twenty or thirty years older, known as
> "the old annex." It was eight stories high, and the street floor was

occupied by shops and a restaurant. To the right was a building of six stories, which was known as "the new annex." . . . The hotel, set in a quarter of the city that was a little remote from the great business and pleasure districts, depended largely for its custom on the patronage of a "permanent" clientele. It was, in short, the kind of place often referred to as a "quiet family hotel" — a phrase which the management of the Leopold made use of in advertising. . . . The Hotel Leopold . . . housed within its walls all of the barren and hopeless bitterness of a desolate old age. For here — unloved, friendless, and unwanted, shunted off into the dreary asylum of hotel life — there lived many old people who hated life, and yet who were afraid to die.

Most of them were old people with a pension, or a small income, which was just meagrely sufficient to their slender needs. Some of them, widowed, withered, childless, and alone were drearily wearing out the end of their lives here in a barren solitude. Some had sons and daughters, married, living in the city, who came dutifully to stamp the dreary tedium of waning Sunday afternoons with the stale counterfeits of filial devotion.

The rest of the time the old people stayed in their rooms and washed their stockings out and did embroidery, or descended to the little restaurant to eat, or sat together in one corner of the white-tiled lobby and talked.[61]

Despite his pictures of beating his knuckles bloody on the walls of his "cell" out of loneliness or despair, Wolfe was comfortable enough at the Albert. He worked out an arrangement with the clerks at the desk in the lobby to cash his checks, lend him money, and extend credit to him at the end of the month until he got his salary on the first. On one occasion he had a tiff with the manager who did not understand the arrangement that his underlings had made; Wolfe privately cursed him in a letter to his mother (asking her to cover a draft) as a "way-down Easter from Maine" with "a low-down, suspicious, get-the-money instinct." The manager apologized "profusely," and Wolfe stayed on.[62] In the course of the year he himself was instrumental in making the hotel much more trouble than the hotel made him. According to his account, he introduced a wastrel friend from Carolina who had been living at the Yale Club but now moved into the Albert. A short time later the friend got very, very drunk and set fire to his room. Because the friend paid for the damage he had done, the matter was dropped.[63]

In his first term at Washington Square College, Wolfe did little but devote himself to his teaching. "During the past four or five months," he wrote his mother in June, "I have broken away from everything and everybody."[64] He was vexed that Professor Baker did not write,[65] but Koch, who was putting together the second series of *Carolina Folk Plays*, had looked in upon him in March and asked permission to print the "Return of Buck Gavin."[66] Wolfe was reluctant to let Koch print the one-acter, for not only had Koch failed to include it in his first series, but Wolfe saw now its crudity and doubted if he could afford to have it appear under his name. He assented later, apparently, after Koch appealed by mail and wire.[67] From February to June, however, Koch's visit was his only real break from routine, save some attendance at the theater.[68] His classes absorbed all his time and energy. Not only did he find the work of correcting papers "interminable," but preparation for his classes and meeting them were utterly exhausting. "On my teaching days I am so worn by nightfall that I sleep as though drugged. I don't know how to conserve nervous energy. I burn it extravagantly."[69]

Wolfe had anticipated that one of the rewards of his teaching would be the acquirement of new and rich literary materials from the East Side. Three days after he began to teach he wrote Mrs. Roberts: ". . . The students, moreover, mainly Jewish and Italian, have come up from the East Side; many are making sacrifices of a very considerable nature in order to get an education. . . . I expect to establish contacts here, to get material in my seven months' stay that may prove invaluable. . . ."[70] What he did not anticipate was that his students would expect to get from him more than he was prepared to give, such was their hunger to learn. At the University of North Carolina, Wolfe had been, like most American undergraduates in the early twentieth century, completely oblivious to the passion for learning. He was probably quite complacent about that part of the caption beneath his picture in *Yackety-Yack*, the senior annual for 1920, which reads, "He can do more between 8:25 and 8:30 than the rest of us can do all day, and it is no wonder that he is classed as a genius."[71] John Livingston Lowes later impressed him with his learning — the Harvard scholar was then working on *The Road to Xanadu* — and may have been partially responsible for starting Wolfe off on his exaggerated orgies of reading in the Widener Library[72] and for his later boasts of omnivorousness, but there is no indication that he stimulated in Wolfe a desire for that organized and consistent study which is genuinely fruitful of knowledge. Tom Wolfe acquired no real discipline at Harvard; even his Workshop accomplishment was slight in view of the long time he was there,[73] and he lacked both method and substance when he began to teach.

But on alternate days he faced — with scarce interval enough to prepare himself either intellectually or psychologically — the most eager learners in the entire American academic world. They were not all from the East Side, as we have seen, but from the five boroughs and the suburbs, nor were they mainly Jewish and Italian, as Tom told Mrs. Roberts: most were children of the lower middle class of all creeds, races, and nationalities — a fine cross section of second-generation Americans with whom the recollection of poverty and lack of opportunity was fresh enough and sufficiently vivid to provide a tremendous spur to learning. Even more eager to assimilate all that their teacher could give them were the many youngsters who were earning part or all of their own way. Thirty years with their economic changes and population shifts have brought New York University a student body indistinguishable from that of any other large institution, but they have not wiped out the memory of those classes of the twenties with their eager listeners and their earnest inquirers. One looked forward to each encounter with them, one wished return engagements, so to speak, but the sessions could be as strenuous and as depleting as an athletic contest to which one gave everything one had. Though many students had inherited from their Old World parents an immense deference for the lowest academic titles and raised no objections and posed no questions, there were a noisy and persistent few who were no respecters of persons and who felt the strongest motivation to realize fully upon their investment in higher education. They may not have had sufficient background to ask the right questions, but the wrong ones could reveal as awkward a deficiency in a young teacher, not only to his embarrassment, but to that also of his student sympathizers. The prodigious curiosity of the vociferous few constantly demanded an *explication des textes* before that sort of exercise became fashionable. Discussion was apt to involve in the end most of the students, the silent eventually taking sides if there were an issue, wherever good sense, rather than diplomacy or manners, prompted them. They were an engaging lot, devoted and impetuous, as capable of discharging electricity as a Leyden jar. Even in composition it was never enough to tell them to do something; someone would feel a Baconian urgency to ask "Why?" And it was impossible before the hour to anticipate what questions they might ask.

Wolfe came to face them with dread, if not terror. Though he exploited a natural fluency probably sharpened in debate, they forced an admission from him by June that "I am not and never will be a schoolteacher."[74] The bell at the end of the hour brought no release, no surcease from their questioning. They merely crowded around the teacher's desk and all seemed to ask questions at once:

> At the end of each class, jostling, thrusting, laughing, shouting and disputing, they would surge in upon him in a hot, clamorous, and insistent swarm, and again, as Eugene backed wearily against the wall and faced them, he had the maddening sense of having been defeated and overcome. . . . The class brought to him only a feeling of sterility and despair, a damnable and unresting exacerbation and weariness of the spirit, a sense of having yielded up and lost irrevocably into the spongelike and withdrawing maws of their dark, oily and

insatiate hunger, their oriental and parasitic gluttony, all of the rare and priceless energies of creation.[75]

The agony that his unconscious inquisitors caused the future novelist aroused a fury in him which he focused especially upon his Jewish students. They probably did ask the most searching questions, but to understand why he concentrated on them requires a deeper penetration. Wolfe seems to have been mastered by an anti-Semitism of which at times he was partially, but only partially, aware. In his moments of awareness he fought this and did some notable things to demonstrate publicly a lack of prejudice, like selecting Jewish students for his typists and taking aggressively the part of a secretary in the Department of English whose Roman Catholic husband had left her, as Wolfe believed, at the urgency of a bigoted mother. The most notable example, of course, of his desire to appear unprejudiced is the expression of indignant sympathy, in *You Can't Go Home Again*, for the little Jew whom he saw trying unsuccessfully to escape from Hitler's Germany. But passages in his novels and the recollections of friends leave no doubt of a deep-seated hostility to the Jews. Possibly this was in a degree self-defensive — a reaction to a fear that he himself might be taken for a Jew. The name Wolfe (with variant spellings) is common among Jews, and his dark hair, rather full lower lip, and "city pallor" may have heightened the impression. His hardly conscious anti-Semitism is revealed not merely directly in his portraits of some of his students but indirectly in such things as his hatred and fear of New York, his unusual sense of loneliness there, and his desire to provide himself, in whatever fictional guises in his novels, with an indisputable Anglo-Saxon ancestry. In *Of Time and the River*, however, he attempts to justify his portraits of his Jewish students on the basis of their terrifying inquisitiveness. The women appear to have filled him with even more terror than the men; that winter had sharpened an appetite for the flesh,[76] and he was much too conscious now of the sex of some of his students. This was the

Jazz Age, never forget, and if the girls at Washington Square were not the same as those that disturbed the boys in the raccoon coats at Williams and Princeton, they could emulate their more self-conscious and sophisticated sisters. But their conduct at worst was purely imitative; at heart they were more innocent than choirboys. Nevertheless they disturbed Tom excessively and in a notorious passage in *Of Time and the River*[77] Eugene accuses them of deliberately arousing erotic impulses in their teacher by cleverly contrived contacts and calculated "shamelessness" and "indecency." The gross exaggeration of this incredible passage can only be explained by the emotional state of the author.

One student more than all the others engaged his attention — a boy in his eleven o'clock class whom he calls Abe Jones in *Of Time and the River*.[78] Jones's intelligence at once made him more aware of Wolfe's limitations (or Wolfe thought it did) and placed him more securely beyond the reach of his instructor's retaliatory powers than did the native endowment of any other student. Because he became symbolic of what Wolfe assumed to be the desire of his students to expose him, Wolfe unconsciously came to hate him. To emphasize his own fatigue he transfers Abe in the novel from the eleven o'clock class to an evening class, which he did not have in his first year at the College.

> ... At this final, fagged, and burned-out candle-end of day, Abraham Jones, as restless as destiny, would be there waiting for Eugene. He waited there, grim, gray, unsmiling, tortured-looking behind an ominous wink of glasses, a picture of Yiddish melancholy and discontent, and as Eugene looked at him his heart went numb and dead; he hated the sight of him. He sat there now in the front rows of the class like a nemesis of scorn, a merciless censor of Eugene's ignorance and incompetence: the sight of his dreary discontented face, with its vast gray acreage of painful Jewish and involuted intellectualism, was enough, even at the crest of a passionate burst of inspiration, to curdle his blood, freeze his heart, stun and deaden the fiery particle of his brain, and thicken his tongue to a faltering, incoherent mumble. Eugene did not know what Abe wanted, what he expected, what kind

of teaching he thought worthy of him: he only knew that nothing he did suited him, that the story of his inadequacy and incompetence was legible in every line of that gray, dreary, censorious face.[79]

Did Tom but know it, Abe asked questions that were being asked instructors in every section of English Composition, where they were not suppressed by a torrent of Southern rhetoric and the awesome masculine force of the instructor. Abe merely penetrated by indomitable persistence his instructor's almost invulnerable defenses. "Why didn't Eugene give them better topics for their themes? Why didn't they use another volume of essays instead of the one they had, which was no good?[80] Why, in the list of poems, plays, biographies and novels which Eugene had assigned, and which were no good, had he omitted the names of Jewish writers such as Lewisohn and Sholem Asch? Why did he not give each student private 'conferences' more frequently, although he had conferred with them until his brain and heart were sick and weary. Why did they not write more expository, fewer descriptive themes; more argument, less narration?"[81] Here is no question that might not legitimately be asked, and if Washington Square College students do not ask them today it is not only because they are not so well motivated as were their predecessors but also because the faculty itself has learned to ask some of these questions of itself.

In *Of Time and the River* Wolfe tells how he turned on this student and bullied him into tears. The boy had never said he did not like Wolfe's class — in fact, he considered it the best class he had, as did all the other fellows. Placated, Wolfe reconsidered Abe Jones and "suddenly . . . began to like him very much." Admitting the boy to terms of intimacy, he was given his golden opportunity to learn about East Side life when Abe invited him into his home to meet his family. For this hospitality Wolfe paid off with the most vicious satire. The name "Jones" had been conferred by an immigration inspector who could not understand the Yiddish patronymic of Abe's father; Abe by "the same theft and rape" had taken the name "Alfred" and was signing himself "A. Alfred Jones" at this time. "Was he using the mails in some scheme to swindle or defraud?" Wolfe asks. "Or was it part of a gigantic satire on Gentile genteelness, . . . a bawdy joke . . . ?" Though Abe had five brothers and two sisters, Wolfe concentrated on Abe's most devoted sister for extended portraiture. He reports her devoid of maternal feeling, cynical and hard toward her child; her attention was focused on her own dress and her jewelry. Discovering that Abe carries on a "correspondence" with a former school chum in the next block, Wolfe makes that also a subject for merciless satire, implying in the end that a homosexual attraction stimulated it. In fact, the whole treatment of Abe and his family is a smear, modified by pretensions of friendship and understanding.[82]

Despite Wolfe's impression that he submitted to a barrage of questioning, there is not much evidence to show that his classes afforded great opportunity for an exchange of opinion or that Wolfe reached terms of intimacy with many of his students. By nature a monologuist and passionately fond of rhetoric, Wolfe indulged in his own opinions or read to his students during a large part of every period. Incidentally, it is those teachers who are enamored of their own voices who most resent questioning. A. Gerald Doyle, who was in one of his last classes, remembers Wolfe as "surcharged with energy and with a bursting love of words. He spewed words which couldn't come fast enough for his seething brain. He reminded us at the time of a passage in Boswell's *Johnson* which described the old rip as a man who ate like a tiger and drank his tea in oceans. We forget the exact wording of the passage, but it always brings Wolfe to mind, and not because of meat and tea. It is the bursting, bumbling impact of the man that's suggested."[83] Though he supplies more detail, Theodore G. Ehrsam's recollections merely strengthen the impression of the monologuist:

> . . . When he spoke to the class on poetry, for instance, (the text used in the course was Watt & Munn's *Ideas and Forms in English and American Literature*) whether about *Beowulf* or Thomas Hardy's

"Hap," he seemed to be entranced, intrigued with the beauty of language, of literature, of love. Up and down the front of the long room would he stride in long, jerky steps, holding the bulky volume in one of his huge hands while he recited poetry; though he held the book open, he rarely had to read, for many of the poems he knew by heart. . . . On some days in class, Mr. Wolfe would be more than usually enthusiastic. Then his eyes would shine, his cheeks would flush, his voice would quiver with emotion, his head would toss almost wildly in emphasis of his words and his lower lip would, in his sheer excitement, become flecked with bits of foamy white saliva. At moments like these, when he wasn't looking directly at us, a few of us students would nod sagely to each other, wink, and whisper, in our crude lack of understanding. "He's off again on another one of his sprees!" But we didn't dare interrupt his almost magical flow of words; we had an uncomfortable feeling that inspiration of some sort had seized hold of him, though we were never articulate enough to say this to each other . . . .[84]

The procedure varied sometimes when Wolfe asked the class to read in turn stanzas from a long poem or make oral book reports,[85] and there were the interruptions. Catherine Ruth Smith recalls one of these:

I have an anecdote of Thomas Wolfe, . . . and my memory of it is so clear that I could swear to every word. He was my English teacher when I first came to the University as a student in 1925. One day we were doing poetry and he was discussing a number of Tennyson's poems, and among them he mentioned, in fact he read, "As Through the Land At Eve We Went," and he said it was a rather "slight" poem. Now this was an Education class, and we were of all ages, and a man somewhat older than most of us, sitting toward the back of the room, spoke up and said: "Mr. Wolfe, may I suggest that those who have lost a child would not regard this as a slight poem." There was a kind of electric feeling in the room at his words, he spoke so very sincerely, obviously out of personal experience. Thomas stopped short and was silent a moment, and then he exclaimed: "You're absolutely right!"[86] I did enjoy and profit by his teaching so much.

Professor Albert S. Pegues, now retired, during one term had a classroom near enough to the one occupied by Wolfe and his class to know something of what went on:

> ... I do recall that his classroom was near mine and that quite a hubbub went on before Tom got into his lecture. I can see him now standing, great giant of a man with a great shock of coal black, disheveled hair, with hands on desk and shouting, "Order, quiet, please!" But, as I recall, there was really never much order or quiet in his room. I can hear him lecturing away in his pell-mell, tumultuous way, with an occasional lull when he seemed to be reading some poem. The whole performance was like a soapbox affair, it seemed to me.[87]

Tom Wolfe was one of the severest markers who ever taught at Washington Square College. In his first semester he gave only three A's to his 104 students, sixteen B's, fifty-three C's, twenty-one D's, nine F's, and two "Absent" marks when only grades of C or better counted as credits for graduation. In his last semester, when he had 101 students, he gave only one A, eight B's, forty-five C's, thirty-one D's, and sixteen F's. Thirteen names scored off the lists indicate that this number of students dropped out of the courses during the semester. These two sets of reports are typical of Wolfe's grading while he was on the teaching staff of the College.[88] Severe grading is usually indicative of one of two things: high standards, with little sense of student capacity, or irritation because the students have not absorbed what has been presented to them, generally because of ineffective teaching. Neither inference credits Wolfe with much compassion for his students. Even though he wrote Mrs. Roberts in May 1924, "My little devils like me,"[89] there is not much evidence that he reciprocated very strongly their feeling. Indeed, at times he was very bitter toward them, writing, "I have worked too hard, giving my brain and my heart to these stupid little fools; talking like an angel or a god in language too few of them will understand."[90] The same conscience that drove him to mistaken eloquence and through the torture of careful theme reading probably was responsible for his rare overtures to his students. In Ehrsam's year he shocked some of them in a coed class by a wholesale invitation to visit his lodgings. "Come up to visit me in my garret. It's only a hole in the wall, but it's comfortable."[91] In the main, he was too preoccupied with his own affairs to give them other than official attention.

Wolfe's relations with his students, however, were as close as were his relations with other members of the Department of English. In his first year the department was located, with most of the faculty, on the second floor of the Brown Building — a fact of interest in the career of the future novelist since the building stood on the site of the birthplace of Henry James, the greatest writer of fiction America has produced.[92] More important, the members of the department were not housed in separate offices or cubicles, but were in a large open room, seated at double desks, the occupants of which faced each other so that acquaintance was inevitable and a kind of familiar democracy the order of relationship. Later, when the department was moved to the second floor of the Main Building after the American Book Company vacated it, the same order prevailed, save that the department had now grown so large that it had a huge room to itself — as it does today in another building. Because such an office is noisy, the members use it only while waiting for classes or during conferences with students; theme correcting and class preparation are done elsewhere, usually at home. Wolfe himself seems to have done all his work outside the University. The practice of scheduling an instructor's teaching on the fewest number of days, on a Monday-Wednesday-Friday or Tuesday-Thursday pattern, also leads to diminished use of the office, with a resulting casualness in relationships. Many members of the department commute, either to Long Island, Connecticut, Westchester, or New Jersey, and did in Tom Wolfe's day, as he was well aware,[93] and are always anxious to return to their books and their families. Nevertheless the office is a great arena of friendship and always has been. In Tom's day, because the entire staff was young and, in the main, lusty, and because some sense of unconventional adventure pervaded the whole enterprise, friendships were swift, noisy, and demonstrative.

The author of this essay, who came to the College the year after Tom, knows of no cliques or groups within the department whom the future novelist could have resented. He himself knew Tom, whom he thought a shy person despite his oracular and inclusive tendencies when he talked, and it is the author's impression that he made the advances that led to acquaintance. He never became intimate with him through sheer want of time, for he had a wife and baby in the distance, and he was trying to do research in addition to working for his doctorate at Columbia. This kind of existence was common enough and, since it led to preoccupation, might have given the impression of aloofness, did not impulse and the very atmosphere of the department tend against it. The author and Tom frequently passed the time of day, and he was present on some of the infrequent occasions when Tom held forth, to an audience of more than two or three, on his views. There may have been some good-humored baiting, but it was not generally indulged in, and it was never concentrated exclusively on one person. The author can remember specifically one occasion when, in the early evening of a spring night, Tom held us all respectfully spellbound. Through the intercession of a doctor friend he had been witness at the birth of a child in a nearby hospital — probably St. Vincent's — and was much shaken up and excited by what he had seen. But he so volubly and eloquently described the event that we had a sense of greater participation, perhaps, than if we had been present. After *Look Homeward, Angel* appeared, Tom surprised the author one evening by stopping him on the stairs and apologizing, shyly and awkwardly as a child would, for not giving him the book, the publisher had allowed him so few presentation copies.[94]

In view of Wolfe's early declaration in regard to his colleagues ("I liked the men"[95]) and the general atmosphere of good will which prevailed in the department, it was, and is, surprising to find in all of his autobiographical use of his teaching experience his sense that the attitude of others toward him was venomous and the very air in which everyone moved freighted with malice. At the "School for

Utility Cultures" where he worked, he avers in *The Web and the Rock* that he knew only "grievances and annoyances, the surliness of nincompoops and the stupidity of fools, the tissue of paltry intrigues, envies, venoms, gossips, rumors, and petty politics that poisoned the life" of the place.[96] In contrast to the million "rats of the flesh" that prowled the city streets at night, he tells us in *Of Time and the River*, he worked by day "in the weary and hatred-laden air of the university," fronting "the venomous faces of the rats of the spirit."[97] In *You Can't Go Home Again* he remembers the piddling instructors of the "School for Utility Cultures" as shoddy aesthetes without talent.[98] The attack is leveled at one teacher in particular in *Of Time and the River*: "a creature with a wry lean face, a convulsive Adam's apple, a habit of writhing his lean belly and loins erotically as he spoke, and a mind of the most obscene puritanism, who was employed to oversee the methods and work of the instructors . . . ."[99] This is recognized at Washington Square as the grossest kind of caricature of a generally revered professor, who, from 1925 on into the early thirties, had charge of the work in Freshman Composition. A soldier in World War I and student at the Sorbonne, Wolfe's victim is known for the sane outlook toward literature and life typical of the representatives of French culture — in no sense is his mind tinged with "obscene puritanism."[100] In whatever sexual fantasies Wolfe indulged, erotic belly writhing must have been a frequent symbol, he so readily attributes it to others — the tendency is not only demonstrated in this instance but is illustrated in his caricature of the young girls who were his students. It happens, however, that the motivation for the insulting caricature is well known at Washington Square. When *Look Homeward, Angel* appeared, Wolfe asked the man, who was teaching the Novel in the College, for his opinion of the book; he gave him a judicious and tempered criticism, but it cut like the teeth of a saw into Wolfe's spirit. Wolfe retaliated in this cleverly unfair assault, beyond the reach of libel unless the victim admitted a part of the representation.[101]

33

Using this attack as a clue, we may assume that Wolfe's whole attitude toward the department was determined by its response to the publication of *Look Homeward, Angel*. That is, he ascribed to a six-year off-and-on association the inadequate reaction, as he felt, of some members of the department between the publication of the novel on October 18, 1929, and his retirement from the College after turning in his grades from his last examination on February 6, 1930 — a period during which he talked constantly about the book and nothing else and even sought to induce his students to purchase autographed copies.[102] He had driven himself to exhaustion to finish the novel, to cut it and get it in shape, and to read the proofs so that he was in no state to judge temperately the attitude of his colleagues. We must remember that his condition so closely approached dementia at this time that he quarreled with the person who, more than anyone else, Max Perkins even, was responsible for his finishing the book.[103] It is doubtful if anyone in the department responded with jealousy and envy to the publication of *Look Homeward, Angel* — some refused the awe and the accolades that the author expected.[104] Nor can these few be blamed, for some of them were either acquainted with established authors or had themselves already published work of merit in which Wolfe had never displayed the slightest interest — Eda Lou Walton and Léonie Adams in verse, E. B. Burgum and William Troy in criticism, and Vardis Fisher in the novel, for example. It is fairest to all to state that their attitude was probably that of restrained interest. One swallow does not make a summer, nor does a first novel establish the immortality, though it may expose the genius, of its author. There was the general feeling that the success of any one member of the department advanced the prestige of all,[105] and probably far more people congratulated Wolfe than neglected to do so. The author of this essay remembers feeling very happy about the event and seeming to understand and sympathize with Wolfe's enduring agitation, his shaking hand and trembling lip.[106]

One thing is beyond cavil, the frustration to writing that working as a teacher resulted in exacerbated Wolfe's soul and was chiefly responsible for the bitterness he felt toward the College. Speaking of his writing, he says in *The Web and the Rock* that "he would work day and night, almost without pause except for the necessities of the school, and *the time so spent he resented bitterly.*"[107] This exasperation all but swallowed him — he came to hate not only his students, his fellow teachers, but even the buildings. "He hated the building more than he had ever hated any building before: it seemed to be soaked in all the memories of fruitless labor and harsh strife, of fear and hate and weariness, of ragged nerves and pounding heart and tired flesh . . . ."[108] Had he been able to organize and discipline his life, he might have made time for writing, as others have, but his life was no more organized and disciplined than his writing. He sought to triumph over all obstacles by a prodigal use of energy and, being fortunate in securing some organization and discipline from others, both in his life and work, achieved what seemed a success from his method, though perhaps it should be regarded as a spendthrift wastage of a splendid endowment.

His first two terms of employment in Washington Square College resulted in practically no creative work, nor could they have been expected to, since he had to learn the whole business of teaching.[109] The only signal dissipation he allowed himself was a Fourth of July week end at the estate of the parents of Olin Dows at Rhinebeck on the Hudson.[110] Dows, a young painter whom Tom had got to know at Harvard, had moved into the Albert to be near Tom, of whom he was genuinely fond. Tom used the material of this visit for a long section of his narrative in *Of Time and the River.*[111] Toward the end of July he wrote his mother that he had written "a great play — the new one. . . . I have a prolog, two acts, and part of the third finished."[112] He conveniently fails to name the play to her, for she would have realized that it was the same one he had begun at Harvard and had promised to have done the previous summer. But in *Of Time and the River* he names it as *Mannerhouse,* gives an outline of its plot, and tells of reading it at Rhinebeck.[113] Probably whatever he did on it was in May when he wrote Mrs. Roberts that he was working on "one of the finest plays you ever saw" and for the first time acknowledged that the desire to write affected him like "a crude animal appetite."[114] But the fit did not last and probably resulted only in tinkering on what was already written. He submitted "Welcome to Our City" to Alice Lewisohn through an intermediary for consideration for production at the Neighborhood Playhouse in Grand Street which Miss Lewisohn and her sister supported. After considering Wolfe's play, she and her directors decided against doing it. Word reached Wolfe later that she said they would have done the play if Wolfe were not the "most arrogant young man" she had ever known.[115]

Early in April he had written his mother of his intention to go abroad as soon as his second term was over in September. He felt that he could live in England very cheaply and devote himself wholly to writing. He would have five months' pay coming to him on the first of September and he might be able to persuade the University — as instructors were constantly doing — to pay him in a lump sum.[116] It would not be much of a gamble — he could return to teaching if he did not immediately succeed, though he did not wish to.[117] He had done well enough as a teacher so that at the end of his first term Dr. Watt had urged him to continue.[118] But Wolfe stuck to his plan; after his teaching was done, he took passage for England, sailing on the "Lancastria" from New York on October 25.[119] Shortly before sailing he made a resolve to write fifteen hundred words a day every day while he was abroad.[120] Wolfe passed the month of November in England and then went to Paris. Here he had stolen from him, on the third day he was in town, a dilapidated old bag containing the manuscript of the uncompleted *Mannerhouse*. He locked himself in his room (metaphorically) and completely rewrote the play, finishing this task about January 3, 1925.[121] On New Year's Eve he met Kenneth Raesbeck, who had been Professor Baker's assistant in the 47 Workshop, and made the acquaintance of the two ladies who were to accompany them on a motor tour of southern France — the foursome eventually to furnish some of the materials for the Starwick-Elinor, Gant-Ann episodes in *Of Time and the River*.[122] Wolfe, who had been receiving some money from his mother, applied for more in order that he might not have to "sponge" off these people during the trip. All readers of the novel know how this traveling foursome was broken up when the women were not as disgusted as was Eugene Gant at Starwick's homosexual proclivities. But the actual parting may have been due to far less sensational causes; for example, to Wolfe's unwillingness to have his expenses paid by others. After the breakup, if the chronology of the novel is to be trusted and the *Letters to His Mother* seems to support it, Wolfe dashed off to Chartres and then went to Orléans (really Tours?) where he met the horse-blood-drinking Countess whom he has immortalized and who helped him financially so that he could get back to Paris.[123]

Meanwhile Dr. Watt had anxiously been trying to reach him, for there appears to have existed a tacit understanding that Wolfe might return in time to teach in the February-June term of 1925. On November 18, 1924, Watt wrote Wolfe, using the Asheville, North Carolina, address, to offer him an appointment as an instructor in English from February to September at a salary of $2,000 — an increase of $200 over his previous compensation.[124] Either this letter was not immediately forwarded (his mother was in Miami) or it was delayed in transit, for Wolfe never acknowledged it. But anticipating some such letter, Wolfe himself wrote a gossipy note to Professor Watt, telling about the loss of the "prolog and two acts in manuscript of the play I had lived with for more than a year," about completely rewriting it, and about his intention to go on an automobile tour with some "very charming friends." Although his own money was nearly gone, he felt that his mother would help him; at any rate, he believed that what was happening to him was so very important that he did not wish to interrupt it — he would not be available for a February to September teaching schedule.[125] Though this letter is dated January 15, it may not have been posted on that date, unless it, too, was held up in passage, for it came so late to Dr. Watt that he was placed in difficulty, probably, to find a substitute at the last moment for Tom for whom he had held the place open. This substitute was Tom Wolfe's devoted friend and later his designated biographer, John Terry.[126] Terry had been at the University of North Carolina with Wolfe, where he had preceded him on *Tar Heel*; since his graduation he had taken his master's degree at Columbia and had done editorial work in New York City; he was at the time working as coeditor for an organization known as the Children's Book Club. This substitute appointment was the beginning of a long career in Washington Square College for John Terry, where he taught chiefly evening students, was a student adviser, gave a course in Biography and Autobiography, and founded the Thomas Wolfe Biography Club. After Wolfe's death, he was chosen by the family and Maxwell Perkins, Tom's literary executor, to edit *Thomas Wolfe's Letters to His Mother* (1943).[127] Despite evidence, early and late, of John Terry's devotion to Wolfe and his joy in the latter's success, Wolfe made him an object of ridicule, as Jerry Alsop, in *The Web and the Rock*. To no one, however, did Terry ever show that he was hurt by the portrait; he never alluded to it and he never qualified his praise of Tom.

After filling the position he had kept open for Tom, Professor Watt still bore him in mind and on February 24, 1925, wrote him another letter generously offering him a teaching position in the regular session, starting the following September and running to June. The pay was to include the raise that would have been his had he accepted the February appointment. Somewhat tardily Watt warned Wolfe jocosely about feminine traveling companions in France, and then recalled an experience of Wolfe's that has become legendary at Washington Square. Accompanied by her mama, one of Wolfe's students had gone to the Hotel Albert with the intent of prevailing through their combined tears upon the young instructor to raise the D— grade he had given her to something better. The management, faced by two weeping ladies in the lobby, had put an obvious interpretation to their visit, and Wolfe's explanation had to be more copious than the tears before the management joined him in getting the women to leave. At the end of his letter Watt urged Tom most warmly to return: "Please do come back, Wolfe. Since you left we have had no one to keep the elevator boys in their proper places and we miss your diminutive form in the faculty room. Send me a letter special delivery and say, 'Thanks, I'll be back'." [128]

Tom found Dr. Watt's letter on his return from his adventure with the Countess and wrote his mother in jubilation about it on March 16, 1925, but he did not immediately reply to it; on April 20, 1925, Watt wrote a "follow-up" requesting a cabled reply. [129] Wolfe had accepted an invitation to visit a North Carolina professor who was staying at St. Raphael in southern France with his family and apparently decided to postpone his reply until he had gone there. [130] Actually he seems to have been delayed a little in reaching St. Raphael, but some time after April 14 [131] he sent Dr. Watt a long letter of grateful acceptance. [132] His family desired him to return in August; hence he accepted with deepest gratitude the post in September. He expressed regret for the confusion that had resulted when he had not been on hand for teaching in February and thanked Watt for his lasting patience with him and kindness to him. Yet, though he accepted the appointment, he wished the acceptance to be regarded as rather tentative for a while, if Watt could permit that: there was a slim chance that he could avoid returning to teaching and could continue to write. [133] With characteristic expansiveness, he sought to differentiate between his desire for creative opportunity and the fantasies of "those wretched little rats at Harvard ... who whine about their 'art' and are unwilling to earn a living." Wolfe had no intention of becoming a "chronic unemployable" of that sort. This led him into a pained and exasperated paragraph on Professor Baker's treatment of him — a topic on which he harped in his letters home during his first year of teaching. [134] The deep hurt of this paragraph explains adequately his retaliation upon Baker

as "Professor Hatcher" in *Of Time and the River*.[135] Wolfe closes
with a reference to his having fallen into the clutches of an aged
Countess at Orléans "who drinks horse blood to revive her fainting
spirits" and a passage on the land of "opulent Springtime" where
he is staying.

There is no reference in the correspondence of Wolfe and Watt
to Watt's follow-up letter, but Watt immediately replied to Wolfe's
last, urging that teaching was no particular handicap to a writing
career and even flattering Wolfe on his eccentricity:

> I believe there is room in a department, especially in New York
> City, not only for excellent teachers and good scholars, but for men
> who have a creative impulse. Indeed, I have a feeling that the depart-
> ment can absorb with profit a reasonable number of temperamental
> gentlemen like yourself who have color and imagination to inspire
> students as well as to teach them.

He went further to tell Wolfe he could cut loose at any time he
wished: "Association in the department here is like a trial marriage
which can be annulled almost at will and without any of the dis-
repute that comes from divorce in social circles."[136] His chairman
could not have indicated to Wolfe any more clearly that he was in
a sense a privileged person at Washington Square, for, as Wolfe
must have known, Dr. Watt was much more rigorous in defining
their obligations to other members of his staff. Wolfe responded,
on June 22, 1925, from Paris with one of the most captivating of his
letters.[137] He would be back before the opening of the term, but he
regretted learning, as he had from Watt's letter, that the latter
would be in California during the coming academic year. "My decision to return was not utterly contingent on your own presence,
but it was considerably strengthened by the expectation of again
working with you." Wolfe had only two requests: that he be relieved
of any registration work and that he have no early morning classes
— no nine o'clocks: "I am incurably and unfortunately night-
owlish, doing a good part of my work when most of the world, even
in New York, is silent, getting Satanic inspirations from the dark."

Waggishly — and in keeping with the temperament Watt had given him — he informed him that he was writing him on paper used by young Frenchmen and women for making assignations. And he tossed in a beautifully turned descriptive sentence or two for good measure. Watt replied on July 16, 1925,[138] acceding to both his requests. Wolfe need not report until September 21; by intuitive appreciation of Wolfe's desires he had already worked out an afternoon program for him:

English 1-2 (D)	M W F	2:00-3:00
English 1-2 (M)	M W F	3:00-4:00
English 1-2 (D)	M W F	5:00-6:00
English 110.3-4	Th	4:15-6:00

In his year abroad Wolfe had had some extraordinary adventures, but more importantly, and allowing fully for his demonstrable tendency to exaggerate on this score, he had done more writing than he had hitherto done in his life. To be sure, he did not write the fifteen hundred words a day he had pledged himself to. He did, however, complete a play, and he did write a long account of his voyage, though perhaps not a short novel.[139] Moreover he had begun, irregularly and unsystematically, to take notes — some of which are published in *Of Time and the River*.[140] The play — *Mannerhouse* — was published from Wolfe's manuscript in 1948 by Harper's. It is an ineffective play which Wolfe himself has characterized well enough in a passage already cited. During the ensuing academic year Wolfe submitted both *Mannerhouse* and "Welcome to Our City" to the Provincetown Theatre and the Theatre Guild, on their request, but neither organization decided on production of Wolfe's work.[141]

Wolfe's greatest adventure of his sojourn awaited him on the boat back to America, for he then met and fell in love with Aline Bernstein.[142] "Esther was fair; she was fair; she had dove's eyes." Mrs. Bernstein, altered in a variety of ways into the Esther Jack of Wolfe's next three novels, though she was seventeen years older than her lover and the mother of two children, was a beautiful, well-poised woman, married to an especially successful business-man.[143] The daughter of Joseph Frankau, a Shakespearian actor who reached the summit of his career playing supporting roles to Richard Mansfield and who is charmingly and affectionately im-mortalized as Joe in *An Actor's Daughter*, Aline Bernstein was taught most of the feminine lead roles in Shakespeare's plays by the same father before she was fourteen. After graduating from the public schools and attending Hunter College in New York City, she both studied and taught in the New York School of Applied Design for Women. She resumed her art work as soon as her children could be entrusted to a nurse, studying painting under Robert Henri. When her friends, Alice and Irene Lewisohn, built the Neighborhood Playhouse as a cultural facility connected with the settlement house in Grand Street, Aline Bernstein became inter-ested in scenic and costume designing. She developed very rapidly as a designer, moving from the amateur to the professional class even prior to the period of her acquaintance with Tom Wolfe, and she has since designed sets and costumes for many Broadway pro-ductions. Turning to fiction first with a book of short stories, *Three Blue Suits* (1933), she has proved herself a competent craftsman in *The Journey Down* (1938), *An Actor's Daughter* (1941), and *Miss Condon* (1947). *Three Blue Suits* contains a portrait of a sleeping young author, called "Eugene," to whose Bohemian quarters his lady love comes bearing all sorts of good things for lunch. When he wakes, he tells her that he has an engagement but that the food will do for dinner, and he reads to her the very poem from John Donne that Wolfe had used to decorate the dedicatory page to "A. B." in *Look Homeward, Angel*; after they have coffee, he dashes off to lunch with his editor. Because he had written all the previous night, he later falls asleep at his uptown club and keeps her and the dinner she has prepared for him waiting. It is only after he has surfeited himself that he confesses to have taken that very day his editor's advice and applied for a Guggenheim fellowship which will carry him away from her — despite all his promises. Their ensuing quarrel ends in tears, regrets, and sleep. *The Journey Down* is an account of a woman's loss of a once violently inflamed young lover, also a writer (and one who has failed in the theater and hates it), of her futile efforts to win him back after an absence, and of her bare retention of life itself in a resulting illness. Here the quarrel of the lovers begins because the heroine thoughtlessly talks of her own trials and successes as a stage designer when the author-lover needs consolation in the fatigue following creative effort. She had "only wanted to show him if he loved me, I was something worthy to be loved, that he was not loving a woman too far below his own great self." But secretly she acknowledges, "My Jewish blood, he hates the Jews." In the most recent and least pertinent of her novels, combining her knowledge of both the world of the studio and the theater, Aline Bernstein tells how a successful Broadway producer forgives his wife for a headlong affair in Italy and a bigamous marriage.

But even when both parties seem to make fictional use of a common experience, and the fiction of one of them is as detailed and specific as that of Tom Wolfe, much remains concealed to the general eye. A comparison of the novels of these two artists, however, would seem to reveal that they were attracted to each other by a shared unusual passion, sensuous in the extreme, for beauty. Both had fathers who spouted poetry.[144] Both had haunted art galleries. Both had an intense love of good food.[145] Both were working for the theater, the one successfully, the other hopefully. Both were extremely knowledgeable on the subject. If mutual interests ever propelled and kept people together — though it has never been proved that they do — their common interests were enough to weld this pair of lovers to each other. But the intellectual attraction was probably as nothing beside the emotional compulsion. Tom Wolfe had just had an affair of "heartbreak"[146] with a woman older than himself in the "Ann" of the novel *Of Time and the River*; that experience taught him that an age discrepancy brought a richer com-

43

panionship, and actual knowledge of his new love revealed a depth he had not encountered hitherto in woman. "His spirit," he wrote, "was impaled upon the knife of love." [147]

Teaching and his love affair probably absorbed Wolfe's chief energies during the academic year 1925-1926. A year's experience made teaching easier for him; on the other hand, he had a new section of Sophomore Literature to prepare for a School of Education class whose older students must have given him some anxiety, and the very good schedule that Dr. Watt had worked out for him had been exchanged for one which involved four days' teaching the first semester and five days' the second.[148] Late changes in schedules are a frequent necessity in a large school when student demand does not develop as anticipated for a given hour. James B. Munn, who administered the department that year in Dr. Watt's stead, had no experience at scheduling and little patience for it; consequently Wolfe's schedule, along with several others, was poor throughout the year. But aside from this Wolfe found in Munn a very appreciative superior. Puckish and ebullient, Munn ran the department like a picnic and was as well disposed toward those who forgot to bring the paper napkins as toward those who made and brought the sandwiches. Son of a very wealthy man who was also a member of the New York University Council, Munn used a large purse to aid indigent students, especially if they took their poverty with some show of gaiety, and an occasional faculty member, if he were not too stuffy. He had been educated at Harvard in the days of sound scholarship and had acquired a curious erudition in widely separated areas, but in general he evaluated scholarship very lightly and was the patron of creative aspirants in the department. It is barely possible that Wolfe read papers for Munn in the latter's English 35-36 course that year, or at least the first semester, when he had a lighter program than was planned, and the two men became intimate. "I taught Types of Literature in the evening that year or the next, and he assisted me," Dr. Munn writes. "I came to know him well, as he was very open-hearted, and we had many talks. He liked

44

to teach in the evening, go back to his room (or rooms) at the Albert on University Place and 8th (?) St., correct his themes, and then settle down to write all night. He slept all day. Anecdotes, I haven't, from that period. We talked much about life, and art and teaching, and writing. . . . To listen to Tom Wolfe was like surf bathing: — the brilliant torrent of words and ideas struck one like a succession of breaking waves and they followed one another so rapidly that I was dazzled, though not deafened. He was very kind, very simple, absolutely loyal, and of the finest integrity. It was not a question of purely abstract intellectual thought, but passionate belief, expressed in language which was always imaginative and poetical."[149] It is good to have Dr. Munn's recollection, for it reminds one of how charming Wolfe could be. Wolfe himself had great affection for Munn and gave him a typescript of *Mannerhouse* when he had one made that year.

The best proof that the love affair was the absorbing interest of 1925-1926 is that Wolfe uses practically none of his college experience of that year in his novels. The episodes are drawn chiefly from his previous experience or from what followed. His mind was not focused especially on his college work. In his first letter to his mother in October of that year, after he had settled in again at the Albert, he describes what proved to be more or less the pattern of his life for the session. He had spent the week end before school started probably at Olin Dows's. Then his 47 Workshop-New Hampshire friend, Henry Fisk Carlton, had been in town, and he had spent several days with him. On the strength of Tom's encouragement, Carlton applied to Professor Munn for appointment to the College staff; Munn hired him on November 4 to begin work in February. Later in the year Tom covered Carlton's classes while the latter's play, "Up the Line," was tried out in Stamford, Connecticut.[150] With such old friends as Carlton and Terry in the city and teaching with him, Wolfe could not complain of loneliness as he had in the past to his mother. In that October letter he also told his mother for the first time about the "very beautiful and wealthy lady, who was extremely kind to me on the boat, and who designs scenery for the best theatres in New York, and supports another with her money." He added that she was seeing him "daily" and entertaining him "expensively." Under the circumstances we can understand why he reported that "it seems I shall have very little time for writing this year."[151] There is no evidence of any literary work of any consequence during the academic year.

Wolfe left New York for France on June 23, 1926, aboard the Cunarder "Berengaria"; he spent ten days in the French capital, then crossed to London; after a week there, he visited Bath, then turned north to explore York and the Lake District. He returned to London, where he spent a month and where, in a little hired room, he began the writing of what was to be *Look Homeward, Angel*. He told his mother that, whether it was published or not, it would be dedicated "to the best and truest friend I have ever had — the one person who has given love, comfort, and understanding to my lonely and disordered life."[152] The novel is dedicated to Aline Bernstein through use of her initials and apt selection of seventeenth-century verse:

> *Then, as all my soules bee,*
> *Emparadis'd in you, (in whom alone*
> *I understand, and grow and see,)*
> *The rafters of my body, bone*
> *Being still with you, the Muscle, Sinew, and Veine,*
> *Which tile this house, will come againe.*[153]

Wolfe had had the idea of writing a novel as early at least as April 4, 1924, when he wrote his mother that "the great novel beats with futile hands against the portals of my brain"[154] and possibly even earlier when he begged her to preserve every one of his father's letters since they very accurately recorded the marble cutter's speech.[155] Probably the event that turned him to fiction was the rejection of both of his plays by the Theatre Guild and the Provincetown during the previous year. Lawrence Langner, of the Guild, had come to the conclusion that Wolfe never would be a dramatist.

"He did not put his play into satisfactory shape. As I met him from time to time, and I read his novels, as big, sprawling and disorganized as their author, I doubted whether he would ever possess the discipline to observe the hard rules which the theatre imposes upon its writers."[156] "Ever" is a long time, and those who are of the opinion that it would be for "ever" before he possessed the discipline to write a successful drama fail to note the sense of form he was developing in small units of his work, as in the "Seven Ages of Man" passage or the magnificent "The Hollow Men" chapter of *You Can't Go Home Again*.[157] Wolfe was swamped by his own abundance, and he obeyed the first impulse of the writer of genius, to let that abundance pour forth; but who is wise enough to say that he could never have channeled and directed it when there is evidence of a growing tendency to discipline himself, after he lost the fear of not expressing himself at all which was always coupled with the fear of early death? While he was in this state the novel was a more natural form of expression, and he instinctively felt his way to it. That he did not abandon utterly the idea of writing for the theater is suggested by the completely flattering, thinly disguised portrait of Theresa Helburn as Miss Heilprinn in *You Can't Go Home Again*.[158] Wolfe realized that Miss Helburn occupied the throne of power in the Theatre Guild and he might need her favor some day.

After a month in London, Wolfe was in Belgium for two weeks; then he returned to England and passed five weeks in Oxford,[159] where he did some more writing. It is possible that at this time he may have had an affair with a young Englishwoman, described in *Of Time and the River* as the daughter of the family with whom Eugene was staying.[160] The episode is moved ahead so that Eugene will not seem unfaithful to Esther Jack (whom he had not then met, according to the novel). But, of course, this episode may be purely fictional. From Oxford he went to Germany for the first time, then returned to the United States on the "Majestic," arriving just before the New Year.[161] He had written Mrs. Wolfe of his intention to return to New York to get employment and had expressed the fervent wish that he would not have to teach again.[162] But he apparently went around to the department office, shortly after arriving, to see if there might not be an opening. There exists a note from Dr. Watt, dated January 3, 1927, in which Watt expresses a desire to see Wolfe about an appointment,[163] and three days later Tom wrote Julia Wolfe that the University people had tried to "sign him up" for two years (not a usual practice), starting with the February session at a salary of $2,200. He added that his "friend"— Aline Bernstein — would stand by him, which can only mean that she offered to support him, until his novel was done.[164] At the time, Tom thought he could finish the book by spring;[165] consequently Mrs. Bernstein prevailed upon him by suggesting that he could pay her back through getting a job in an advertising agency which she would help him to secure.[166] This understanding was necessary for Tom's pride. With Tom, Mrs. Bernstein hired a loft at 13 East Eighth Street[167] for thirty-five dollars a month, and here at the back Tom had his living quarters and wrote while at the front Aline Bernstein had her drafting equipment for her stage work, the skylights overhead furnishing an excellent light. Sex played so large a part in the feelings of the young instructors of the twenties that all who knew about this establishment were more apt to reflect upon its possible illicit aspects than to consider seriously its government and economy. Aline Bernstein brought to Wolfe's daily life regularity and order, beginning with breakfast or "brunch," which she frequently came down and prepared for him. ("Why do you take lunch with me nine days a week?") She kept him at his novel, and for the first time manuscript really began to pile up. Wolfe guarded them against casual intrusion by using the Harvard Club for his address.

On February 5, 1927, Professor Watt wrote Wolfe at the Harvard Club address offering him an appointment as an instructor in the regular 1927-1928 academic year at a salary of $2,200. Watt suggested that Wolfe accept the appointment provisionally in order to be sure of it; he asked to be notified by May 1 if Tom did not wish the post.[168] Wolfe replied from Boston on March 7, 1927, where (he explained) he had gone to recover some volumes of verse he had left with his Uncle Henry some years before when he was a student in Cambridge. His uncle, bereft of his wife, had remarried, taking as his bride a woman forty-four years younger. The enamored pair were in Florida on their honeymoon but Tom, with the aid of a cousin, hoped to gain entrance to his uncle's house and secure his property. Turning to Dr. Watt's proposition, he wrote:

> I know you will be glad to hear that I have worked hard and stead-ily in my garret, and that I hope to have my huge book on paper by May, and in the hands of a publisher (I hope!) by summer. I think you understand that what I want to do with my life is to live by and for my writing. That independence — I had better say that slavery — is the highest desire I have ever known. To hope for it at present is precarious. I thank you again, fervently, for your patience, your kind-ness, and your encouragement. May I assume that if the miracle (of publication and royalty) does not happen, I can have employment in the September division, and if it does, and I am able to go on under my own steam, that I may decently (before the term's beginning) with-draw?

Probably glancing through Watt's letter after he had finished his own, he noted that Watt had indicated the terms under which he could withdraw, but being too tired to redraft his letter, since he had visited Hawthorne's house in Concord that day, he added a postscript to that effect and let the letter go. In it he had also reported that his mail address was still the Harvard Club and he promised to look in on Watt some time during the month,[169] and he probably did.

Aside from the trip to Boston, Wolfe allowed himself — or per-haps better, Aline allowed him — few holidays in the spring of 1927. He was at Olin Dows's in April for a few days and then, when the weather got very warm, he went up to Rhinebeck, where Dows let him use the gatekeeper's lodge.[170] But he kept steadily at work until July when his mentor not only permitted him to go abroad but made it possible for him to do so. By that time he had already decided to return to New York University in September.[171] He also put off marketing his book to that time. Wolfe traveled to Europe on the S.S. "George Washington." After staying in Paris, he went on to Munich and Vienna, writing Dr. Watt a long, gossipy letter on August 11 from the latter city in which he asked for a concentrated evening schedule for the coming year.[172] Of special interest is Wolfe's observation that there was no evidence in Vienna of the bloody massacre which had occurred a short time before his arrival (the police had fired into a crowd of people protesting the miscarriage of justice in the acquittal of a defendant accused of killing a socialist war invalid) and his report that the impending execution of Sacco and Vanzetti was stirring up the bitterest hostility to the United States. These observations could have had only passing interest for Dr. Watt, who was vigorously conservative in politics, but they have importance for the student of Thomas Wolfe as revealing his first faint interest in left-wing activities. Later, in 1934, Maxwell Perkins kept him from injecting "radical or Marxian" ideas into *Of Time and the River,* and some critics have felt that the novelist was in a degree emasculated by his editor's interference.[173] But it is clear that Wolfe did not deeply hold these views, and nothing was removed from any of his books without his assent.[174] From Vienna, Tom went on to Prague and then returned somewhat circuitously to Paris. The author of this essay and his wife, recently arrived in Paris on a fellowship, met Wolfe quite by chance in the Louvre on September 9, the day before he took ship back to America. It was just at closing time — in fact, we were with the crowds moving toward the exits — when we saw Wolfe breasting this human torrent like Leviathan. He insisted that we return with him to the room in which the Italian primitives were shown to share his ecstasy — literal and visible — in the paintings of Cimabue which he had just discovered. One cannot forget his disposal of the uniformed guards of the Louvre — he simply brushed them aside and proceeded on his way. Used, surely, to dealing with eccentrics, they saw that usual methods would not do with him and permitted us all to stay and admire "the greatest picture in the world"— one that, whatever its historical merit, had saints disposed in such a flat and geometric order (with no perspective) as would have elicited a more Twainian summary. We came away in Tom's time and at his leisure in a more empty Louvre than we ever saw again, the Louvre that only the watchmen are privileged fully to enjoy.

Before Wolfe wrote Dr. Watt from Vienna requesting a concentrated schedule, Watt had written him on July 25 to tell him that he had worked out just what Wolfe desired —"really an ideal program";[175] after receiving the Vienna letter, Watt wrote again explaining how he had effected this program and notifying him of the usual department meeting on Monday, September 19, the day before classes began.[176] Dr. Watt had, in truth, worked out a good program, which it is possible to reconstruct:[177]

English 1	M W	8:00-9:20
English 35	T Th	1:00-2:00
English 1	M Th	6:30-7:50
English 1	T Th	8:00-9:20

English 35 was the Washington Square College equivalent of English 110.3 that he had taught for the School of Education in 1925-1926, so that Tom had no new courses to prepare for. He was free on Fridays, Saturdays, Sundays, and Mondays until 6:30 P.M. And on Wednesdays he was free until 8:00 P.M. Inasmuch as the English 1 courses were followed by sections of English 2 at the same hours, and the single section of English 35 was succeeded by an English 36, in the second term,[178] Wolfe had a singularly good program throughout the year if he wished to devote his best hours to writing.

Wolfe appears to have devoted himself chiefly to his novel during the academic year 1927-1928. Aline Bernstein resumed control of his daily regimen; together they leased an apartment, consisting of two enormous rooms, kitchenette, and bath, at 263 West Eleventh Street, for $130.00 a month, or, as Tom tells his mother, for $65.00

apiece.[179] They apparently left Tom's "filthy garret" because Mrs. Bernstein needed a better place to bring her theatrical friends to, since the demand for her work was increasing. She occupied the front parlor and transferred all her art materials there. Her success indubitably made the better quarters possible as well as desirable. Tom had no particular interest in his surroundings or his possessions, save for books and manuscripts. "His various quarters in town," Maxwell Perkins has said, "always looked as if he had just moved in, to camp for a while."[180] Henry Volkening, a fellow instructor in Washington Square College, who often visited the Eleventh Street address, says that "the place was in incredible disorder, as Tom's homes usually were, with a minimum of furniture and with manuscripts and books and hundreds of 'Freshman themes' thrown everywhere."[181] But Tom, if no one else could, could labor in disorder, and with Aline Bernstein's constant encouragement, he pushed the book steadily ahead. To get his manuscript typed, he had to read it aloud to Abe Jones, his former student, who was now serving him as a typist, for his writing was not easily decipherable.[182] He now took up a form of composition peculiarly his own. James B. Munn, who had just become Acting Dean of Washington Square College and with whom Wolfe had renewed relationships, says in part:

> . . . I remember the period when he shifted from writing plays to writing novels. The dramatic form cramped him; the novel did not. I knew that "the novel" (O, Lost!) was about his people. He told me of writing it in ledgers with 7b (?) Venus pencils, and then asked me for a student to type the book. . . . The young man didn't have much to say about the typing except the kind of paper he used. I read the typed draft at Tom's request. It was on punctured unlined paper, filed between butcher's account ledger covers, the papers being held in place by rigid hollow pins, fastened in one board and caught in the other . . . .[183]

This version of the novel, on which he had spent twenty months, was finished toward the end of March 1928,[184] and the manuscript was immediately given Dean Munn to read, who did so promptly.

The dean of Washington Square College (N.Y.U.), who is a young man, a millionaire, an idealist, and a sensitive romantic person, has just finished reading it. He wrote me a magnificently honest letter about it: he was terribly shocked at the pain, the terror, the ugliness, and the waste of human life in the book — he thought the people rose to nobility and beauty only at the end (in this he is terribly wrong!). But he said the book was unique in English and American literature, that if it is published it must be published without changing a word, and that he felt that he had lived with the people in it for years.[185]

"I believe I had something to do with his search for publishers," Munn recalls, "but he soon selected an agent. Then came Scribner's, and . . . I wrote a letter to them — the only time, save one other recently — when I did such a thing. I believe they had decided to print the book, and wanted to know about the author."[186] Munn may have suggested some other publisher, but according to *The Web and the Rock* it was Mrs. Bernstein's acquaintance with one of the partners which led Wolfe to submit his novel to the house of "Rawng and Wright."[187] Not hearing from them for over five weeks, Wolfe wrote to inquire and got a note of rejection the next day; he went up to the publishing house and retrieved his manuscript, unopened, as he believed. This led ultimately to the devastating satire of the publishing firm in the same novel.[188] When he returned to the Eleventh Street place, he probably would have destroyed the manuscript — pitched it into "the garbage pail" or "down the privy"— if Aline Bernstein had not rescued it.[189]

She, snatching up the imperiled manuscript and hugging it to her bosom: "No you won't either! . . . This manuscript's *mine!* . . . Who stood by you all these years, and stood over you, and made you do it, and had faith in you, and stuck to you? . . . If you've got no more faith in it now than to throw it away, I won't let you! . . . I'll save it! . . . It's mine, I tell you, mine!"

If no other speech in *The Web and the Rock* is authentic, this one surely is.

Though in the fictional account *Look Homeward, Angel* was next submitted to "James Rodney & Co." through "Lulu Scudder," a literary agent,[190] a number of publishers appear to have seen the manuscript before it was brought into the house of Charles Scribner's Sons by Madeleine Boyd.[191] On Wolfe's testimony, it was Aline Bernstein, who, after these discouragements, got Ernest Boyd ("Seamus Malone") to read it, and his approval led to his wife's taking it on commission.[192] Madeleine Boyd apparently told Wolfe her terms at the end of May 1928, but he did not turn the manuscript over to her until just before he went abroad in July.[193] Meanwhile he had violently quarreled with Aline Bernstein. Apparently influenced first by outside factors, he had begun to question their relationship. Return to the College in the fall of 1927 had brought Wolfe new associates in a group of younger and more "emancipated" friends. Whereas it is difficult to find many who visited Wolfe in his "garret" on Eighth Street — his attitude then being fearful for and protective of his friend — numerous acquaintances visited the Eleventh Street establishment. Two motives seem to have operated: a desire for companionship of youths, men and women of his own age, and a desire to dramatize himself. The actor in Wolfe has been too much neglected — Koch and some of Wolfe's North Carolina associates have remarked on his love of histrionics,[194] so has one shrewd later observer.[195] From his conversations at the Square, Tom came to realize the picturesqueness, if not grotesqueness, of his living and writing arrangements: the simplicity of the bed, chair, and trestle-table furnishings of his room, the litter of clothes and papers and books — and the half humorous impulse to display himself in this sort of chiaroscuro became irresistible. He did not at first sacrifice his friend to it; reflecting on the vanities of the twenties one can see how the thought of touching off his young colleagues' envy may have been mixed with a lover's pride in displaying his lady when he introduced his friends into the Eleventh Street apartment without explanations while Aline Bernstein was at work there. But the new friends were, as we have said, an irreverent, skeptical lot; whether Wolfe heard them say things or whether he read his own meaning into their exchanged glances is immaterial. He commenced to doubt the relationship, and because he was in some ways very immature he commenced to wonder at the quality of his friend's attachment and that wonder became fatal. Had chance merely put him in the way of a romantic woman when she wanted adventure? Was he a "gulled yokel, the country greenhorn"? How his insecurity prompted these questions! Even her race now counted against her. His most extreme fancy made her the Jewish bait in a corrupt Jewish world to capture the Christian man of genius.[196]

But it is also clear that the quarrel was one expression of Wolfe's slowly-built-up antagonism to Aline Bernstein's fruitful discipline. It is, on the whole, a miracle — for his compulsions were canceled by passages of doubt — that she kept him at work. Some will say that Maxwell Perkins performed the same miracle, but the significance of Aline Bernstein's achievement is that what she accomplished was done on purest faith, whereas Wolfe had a contract with Scribner's and a realizable goal in view when Perkins labored with him. Mrs. Bernstein's own success had been won by self-discipline; when she sought to inculcate that iron law in another, in the very year in which she herself was most successful and he the farthest from it, that other resented and resisted not only the discipline but his friend and her success.[197] Wolfe's rebellion took the form of drink — much drink[198]— and women whom he apparently in the final act of defiance brought to the Eleventh Street place.[199] Aline Bernstein became the victim of anxiety for her protégé and jealousy for her lover.

Once while he was writing *Look Homeward,* Emmet Glore and a girl named ——————, who taught at N.Y.U., and I went to have dinner at Wolfe's place on West 11th St. (or somewhere in that vicinity). We went in a body with Wolfe to a bootlegger on 13th Street, where we bought a gallon jug of rum, then we bought steaks, cooked them in his oven and sat on the floor to eat them. There were no chairs. Two saw-horses, carrying planks, were the only furniture, and these were heaped with manuscript. In the middle of the repast a violent middle-aged woman stormed in. Wolfe took her aside and quieted her. After she left he explained that she was . . . [Mrs. Bernstein], who, on patrol outside his windows, had noticed the shadow of a girl on the blind. She had come up to catch him in the act.[200]

When he went abroad in July it was to escape her — not her love and care — but her discipline. He was completely exhausted, defeated, and discouraged. He had lost his "squeal."[201]

With the first version of *Look Homeward, Angel* completed, Wolfe had written Professor Watt a letter of resignation on April 1, 1928, telling him that he did not wish to accept a teaching appointment at the University, that he was going to try to support himself by writing.[202] He would even do hack writing — stories, articles, advertising[203]— but he would write. He admitted that his decision was a gamble, but he added, penetratingly, "The most reckless people, I believe, are those who never gamble at all." He confessed his own state to be one of complete exhaustion and frayed nerves: "I have felt more tired this spring than at any other time of my life — I have felt, along with the finishing of my book, such damnable weariness of my brain and heart as I did not know existed. I am afraid I have been surly, ill-tempered, unable to join happily with other people." Then he turns to a strongly worded denial that he has ever conducted himself in the department as a privileged person, as a Bohemian, or — referring to Dr. Watt's much earlier letter, "a temperamental fellow," in order to get out of work —"within the trap of my nature I have done all the things I could to fulfill my obligation to you. It would cause me very real distress to think you doubted that. I have been at times a very difficult, a very moody and extravagant person, but I do not think I have been a cheap or common person":

> . . . Once or twice, when I was in a chafed or bitter temper, I have heard some of the young men say that I occupied the position of a privileged character — that I was the departmental "wild oat," and

any laxity or extravagance would be permitted me. Now this, I am sure, was harmless joking, but it touched rawly on me at the time. I think no one knows better than I do my deficiencies as a teacher — among which I would name a lack of orderly arrangement, an extravagant and useless expenditure of energy on all things, and a constant belief in miracles — but please believe that within my limits I have given you honest and faithful service.

Because he believed at the time that he was writing his valedictory in this letter, Wolfe set forth clearly his regard for the University and for Dr. Watt and Dr. Munn. Citing the case of Desmond Powell, who, stricken with tuberculosis while serving as an English instructor, had been treated with extraordinary consideration, Wolfe saw in this treatment another illustration of the fact that "New York University is not simply a group of buildings with elevators. . . . If any *good* distinction ever attaches to my name, I shall be proud to acknowledge my connection with this place — if any *bad* one, I shall keep silent." Recurring to his motivation, he declared that he was leaving teaching not because he disliked it but because he feared that he might come to like it too well. He thought his classes "have got some of the best of me during my three years."

The summer, fall, and early winter of 1928-1929 that Wolfe spent in Europe were possibly the most dissipated of his career, though there are some extraordinary later purple patches. He spent his time, in his own words, "cursing, whoring, drinking, brawling his way across the continent"— dispatching an occasional postcard to his mother.[204] There were some amusing episodes. The author of this essay has heard a story (he trusts it is not apocryphal, but he cannot remember the source) of how Tom, engaged in argument with the owner of a bar in Germany or Austria, became annoyed because with his sweeping gestures he thumped his hands on a brass gas jet run down from the ceiling. Without ceasing to talk, so the story goes, he wound the gaspipe up like ribbon candy and pushed it against the ceiling. The proprietor was too astonished by the event to protest. But eventually one of his escapades put him in the hospital with his nose broken, some teeth knocked out, and his skull split. He took on four Germans during the *Oktoberfest* in Munich "in mud, darkness, and pouring rain," and one of them dealt him terrible blows with a stone beer mug. At that, he might have choked his principal assailant to death had not the latter's wife fallen upon him and clawed him until he had to relax his grip on the fellow's throat. He is frank to admit he got into these brawls because he was "insane with the brooding inversions of my own temper, disappointed and sick at heart because of the failure of acceptance of my book, lost to everyone who cared for me (not even leaving an address), sick with a thousand diseases of the spirit . . . ."[205]

Tom Wolfe sailed from Naples for the United States on December 22, 1928, and arrived in New York on January 2, 1929, "penniless" from his "terrible and wonderful" adventures in Europe.[206] He probably went immediately to New York University or the Harvard Club for his accumulated mail and at one or the other place learned that Scribner's wished him to phone.[207] He did so and was summoned to the publishing house, for Mrs. Boyd had tentatively placed *Look Homeward, Angel* in his absence. Maxwell Perkins has told how Madeleine Boyd almost reluctantly had surrendered the manuscript to him only upon his promise that he would read the whole of it. He started with the brilliantly written episode with which the book originally began, the account of W. O. Gant and his brother and two little boys standing by the road and watching a division of Lee's army march by on its way to Gettysburg, but then ran into a passage of sawdust and put the book aside. But Wallace Meyer, also of the editorial staff, picked up the manuscript and, chancing upon another wonderful scene, communicated his enthusiasm to Perkins, and soon he was reading again, and then John Hall Wheelock took it up, and then others. They were deeply interested in the book, and they reported their interest to Madeleine Boyd and to Wolfe, asking the latter to look in at Scribner's on his return from Europe. Perkins later recalled vividly his first vision of Wolfe as he came in response to his telephone summons:

After some correspondence between me and Wolfe, and between him and Madeleine Boyd, from which we learned how at the October Fair in Germany he had been almost beaten to death — when I realized again that we had a Moby Dick to deal with — Wolfe arrived in New York and stood in the doorway of my boxstall of an office leaning against the door jamb. When I looked up and saw his wild hair and bright countenance — although he was so altogether different physically — I thought of Shelley. *He* was fair, but his hair was wild, and his face bright and his head disproportionately small.[208]

Wolfe has given a long account of his impressions of that first interview with the man who was to supersede Aline Bernstein as his literary mentor and who was to guide him gently but persistently in much the same way.[209] It concluded, after Perkins had shown him a lengthy summary of the changes and cuts he wished made in it, with instructions for him to come in for another conference. This occurred two or three days later, when he learned definitely they would take the book, and he promised to bring them one hundred pages a week. Preceded by a note of acceptance, Madeleine Boyd brought the contract for the book and a five-hundred-dollar advance (less her commission) to Wolfe on January 11, 1929.[210]

Either before or after his first interview Wolfe appeared in the department office at Washington Square and inquired about the prospects for a job in February. Dr. Watt, who was forehanded and probably had filled all positions for the February session, could not promise him anything but did declare his intent to keep him in mind.[211] Meanwhile Wolfe had gone to live in an apartment at 27 West Fifteenth Street, just off Fifth Avenue, which he and Aline Bernstein had taken together. Tom had asked permission of Scribner's to communicate their decision at once to "a very dear friend" even before he received the contract;[212] hence Aline knew about acceptance of the book dedicated to her before anyone else did, even Tom's mother. Toward the end of the month Professor E. Raymond Bossange, in charge of the Department of Architecture in the new College of Fine Arts, wrote Acting Dean Munn asking his help in staffing sections in mathematics and English. On January 28 Munn communicated this request to the chairmen of the respective departments in the College and empowered them to deal directly with Bossange.[213] In the next three days Watt managed to reach Tom, and on January 31, 1929, he sent him with a letter of introduction to Bossange:

> Mr. Wolfe has been a highly successful instructor in my department for a number of years. This year he did not ask for an appointment because he wished to travel in Europe and complete the publication of a novel which has, I am glad to say, just been accepted by Scribner's. Mr. Wolfe is decidedly artistic in taste and temperament, is an excellent composition teacher, and will please your students very much I am sure.
>
> My understanding regarding his relationship with you for this semester is that he will teach one section of English 1, Elementary Composition, from February to June, at a salary of $100 a point, or $300 for the course. Since Mr. Wolfe is not on my staff, his salary will be taken care of directly through your office.[214]

In his last paragraph Dr. Watt covered the several ways in which the course might be continued beyond June, and gave it as his understanding that Wolfe's single section of English 1 would meet on Mondays and Wednesdays from 2:00 to 3:30 P.M. Bossange reported in a brief note, "I was most favorably impressed by Mr. Wolfe who is just the type of man we want."[215] But Watt was not content with this; he talked with Dean Munn about using him as a reader in Munn's Bible class, and Munn assented to this. The arrangement gave Tom another $300.00:

Feb. 1, 1929

My dear chief:

> Thank you for the data about Tom Wolfe. I am going to use him to spell Mr. Beals on my papers because I want to spare his eyes and give Tom a little more money. We'll get him through all right.[216]

Faithfully yours,
James B. Munn

Wolfe plunged immediately into the revision of *Look Homeward, Angel*. One of his first needs was a typist, and Dean Munn suggested to him a student in the Bible class, "Jack" Mandel.[217] To this boy he talked freely about his hopes, his fears, and his prejudices, and the boy recorded in a notebook what Wolfe said. Jack typed while Tom wrote or read papers:

> . . . Those ledgers! Page upon page of illegible script! I would spend hours deciphering a few pages before I could begin to type the material and there were occasions when Wolfe himself could not read what he had written previously. One day, when I was working over one of these passages, I came across a fact that Wolfe had mentioned a few pages back. I called his attention to it and asked him whether he wanted me to type it or not. He looked at me a minute or two before he said anything and then, in a rather irritated tone, he remarked, "Of course include it!" Repetition was not harmful, he thought. If his emotions demanded this repetition at the time he was writing, then the material belonged in the book. As a matter of fact, he was sure that everything a man remembered should be included in his books. Though his editors urged him to discipline himself, to restrain the thousand and one tangential directions his story was taking, he was unable to do so. He would return from a visit to his publishers fuming and fretting because they had removed an entire chapter from his book. Like a chastened youngster, he would grumble for a few days before he conceded that they might be right. Wolfe simply could not bear to see those pages deleted. It was like amputating one of his limbs . . . .[218]

Steadily the work of revision progressed, the author lashing himself and others lashing him. By June 6, 1929, he could report to his mother that the completely revised manuscript was in the publisher's hands and that he was awaiting proofs.[219] By the middle of July he felt he could have a vacation, and he went first to Maine and then to Canada.[220]

In April the College of Fine Arts decided to expand the work in English for the following year by offering two courses, one section of English 1-2 and one section of English 35-36. Watt reported to Dean Munn on April 11, 1929: "It is now planned to have both courses taught by Mr. Wolfe. He seems to be doing very well there. The stipend will be one hundred dollars per semester hour to be assumed by the Department of Architecture from the instructor's total salary." [221] A later communication from Watt to Bossange indicates that the following schedule was planned for these courses: [222]

English 1   W 9:30-10:30 A.M., F 10:30 A.M.-12:30 P.M.
English 35   W 10:30 A.M.-12:20 P.M., F 9:30-10:30 A.M.

Some time after Bossange confirmed this arrangement on May 20, 1929, [223] Professor Watt offered Wolfe full employment for the following regular academic year 1929-1930 at a salary of $2,400. [224]

Wolfe decided to accept the offer — he would not take chances until he learned how the book was received. When he reported for work he learned that, in addition to the two sections already arranged for him in the College of Fine Arts, he was to have a section in Washington Square College of English 1 meeting Monday, Wednesday, and Friday from 2:00 to 3:00 P.M. and another section of English 35 meeting on Thursday from 8:00 to 9:45 P.M. [225] The Fine Arts courses met uptown; hence Wolfe would not be in the department office as much as he had been in earlier years, though more than in the previous spring session. In August *Scribner's Magazine* had published "An Angel on the Porch" to help to build Tom up for the publication of his novel scheduled for October 18. [226] The effect on the department was to give Wolfe prestige with the majority but to make him the object of envy to others. In a highly emotional state as he awaited publication, Tom talked too much about the event, even speculating on his sales and what he would do with the money. One member of the department is reputed to have told him that if he sold a million copies it would mean nothing, for "any book that wins popular acclaim is cheap." [227] As pressure built up in him and his nerves became more frayed, some sort of explosion was inevitable. It came after the appearance of the book, which survived even the tremendous uproar in the newspapers over the stock market crash and was widely and favorably reviewed. [228] According to *You*

Can't Go Home Again, "Mrs. Jack" had the great party at her house on or about October 17, the day before his book appeared, and he broke with her shortly after that.[229] Actually, the party was at another time, and the real break occurred just before Wolfe went abroad on a Guggenheim award.[230] The parting is rationalized in the book, but it is best explained in the same terms as his later break with Maxwell Perkins. The natural object for his explosive wrath should have been Perkins, his recent disciplinarian; he was spared because Aline was available. After the break with Mrs. Bernstein, Perkins "suddenly found himself a banker, a financial adviser, a father confessor, a lender of money, an exorciser of constant black moods of despair, an arbitrator of love affairs, a sartorial and social guide, and an elephant trainer."[231] Wolfe eventually turned on Perkins and lampooned him as Foxhall Edwards, and, although that episode in Wolfe's biography lies beyond the province of this essay, it is illuminating to think of it also as a product of the tension of discipline. Wolfe loved each of these people, as it would be easy enough to show in many ways. Nevertheless he injured them more than an enemy could in his agonized fury.

With the success of his novel, it became obvious that Wolfe would no longer need to teach to support his writing. It now seemed as though his writing would support him. Scribner's gave him an advance of $5,000 on his next book and agreed to dole this out to him at the rate of $250 a month.[232] In view of this Wolfe resigned from the College, his resignation to take effect at the end of January 1930, when the current term was over. To boost the young author, Professor Watt arranged for him to lecture on "The Modern Novel" before the Woman's Club of Glen Ridge on November 1, 1929. He startled the gentle suburban ladies a good deal by his appearance, and lacking a timepiece borrowed a wrist watch from one of his audience. They shuddered when he swept this off the table to the floor with one of his gestures, but no harm was done.[233] Wolfe arranged to repeat this lecture for Dr. Watt on two later occasions, once in February, probably before a group of Engineering students

Watt was teaching in the evening, and on May 2, 1930, in East Orange.[234] Bill Tindall, then a young instructor in the department and a friend of Wolfe's, also tried to boost the novelist:

> I gave the first lecture on Wolfe. At that time I was giving a course in the modern novel at Washington Square. I told Wolfe, being sorry for him, that if he would give me a copy of *Look Homeward* before publication, I would prepare a lecture on it and maybe sell a few copies. I gave the lecture a day or two before publication. I think I sold many copies. . . . The class at which I gave this lecture was an evening class. The students were soon as enthusiastic about the book as I was.[235]

To replace Wolfe, Dr. Watt hired Russell Krauss, a Rhodes Scholar who had held a Penfield Fellowship from the University. Wolfe was so much interested in his students that he insisted that Krauss attend the last session of his class in order to get his "method" of teaching, which, as Krauss discovered, consisted chiefly in reading to them.[236] Before he quit the department Wolfe asked Dr. Watt to support his application for a Guggenheim Fellowship. Dr. Watt wrote the following encomium which he sent to the Foundation on January 7:

> Mr. Thomas Wolfe who is applying for a Guggenheim Fellowship is beyond doubt the most vigorously creative of the members of the English department of Washington Square College. The highly favorable reception of his first novel, "Look Homeward, Angel," has justified the confidence which Dean Munn of this College and I have had in the young man for several years. We knew that before long he would "arrive" in a very substantial way. In his personality and energy there is vigor and largeness which is very rare. His ideas and emotions spring perpetually like an artesian well, and I believe that there is little danger that he will write himself out. Indeed, I have yet to meet an American writer who has the lush fecundity that Tom Wolfe exhibits. He ought to go on with his writing for an [in]definite period, increasing in power with each book. Although "Look Homeward, Angel" is his first published novel, he has been writing continually — I should almost say continuously, for he is a tireless labourer

— for many years, and he is, therefore, by no means a tiro. If the Guggenheim Foundation were to make it possible for this man to cut loose from the routine of teaching and conferring with students, he would continue to gather in Europe, as he has already done to some extent in a truly Bohemian manner, the rich materials for a novel that is certain to be better than "Look Homeward, Angel." I am convinced that his ability has increased from year to year as I have watched him grow, and I believe that he is the type of real genius which the Guggenheim Foundation was established to help develop.[237]

Wolfe was notified on March 10, 1930, that he had been awarded the fellowship for which Dr. Watt supported him.[238]

Wolfe's last communication to Dr. Watt was in behalf of a student to whom he had given an F in English 35. He was willing that the student be given another examination, but Dr. Watt could not accede to such an arrangement.[239] But with his letter Wolfe did not quite drop out of the ken of the University. In February 1935 *Of Time and the River*, with its devastating portrait of the College and of Wolfe's former students and colleagues, was published. It was received with incredulity, astonishment, anger, and grief at Washington Square. How could he who had broken bread amongst us, who had shared our limited fare and small rewards, treat us as he had done? Had he no sense of the betrayal of an enterprise to which he had committed so much of himself — a measure, at least, of others' commitment? But the intellectual, especially the teacher, is curiously compounded; as soon as we had felt our resentment and recognized its propriety, we began to make the teacher's excuses for the incorrigible: Wolfe was genius, he had been dominated by mood when he had written, he had not been conscious of conferring injury, he had meant to transmute what he had reported beyond recognition, the report was surely inconsequential beside the fiction. William Faulkner has written of "the consuming unsleeping appeaseless thirst for glory for which any normal artist would destroy his aged mother," and Wolfe clearly felt that awful thirst. It is understandable that, in the grip of it, friends and acquaintances, students and colleagues, kinfolk and his beloved, became simply materials, like sticks and stones, and were so used.

Perhaps to show that the University was above bearing malice for injury Harry Woodburn Chase, the chancellor of the University, who had known Tom at North Carolina, sent him on October 28, 1935, a poem entitled "Strange Campus" which had appeared in the *Year Book* of the School of Architecture and expressed the hope that Tom would come over to have dinner with him sometime.[240]

In the contrite mood that led Wolfe to will half his property to Aline Bernstein after breaking with her and that also led him to write the deeply moving letter to Maxwell Perkins from his sickbed before he became unconscious, Wolfe replied to Chancellor Chase's overture:

> ... As time goes on, and I have been able to get more detachment and perspective on my years at New York University, I have realized that being there is one of the most valuable and fruitful experiences of my whole life. I can think of no other way in which a young man coming to this terrific city as I came to it, could have had a more comprehensive and stimulating introduction to its swarming life, than through the corridors and classrooms of Washington Square. In April of this year I had the opportunity to revisit the great English university at Cambridge. It is gloriously beautiful, even more so than I had remembered it, but somehow it seemed remote from the life of the world around us and my thoughts kept going back to Washington Square and to all the eager, swarming, vigorous life I knew there, and it seemed to me without making comparisons, that whatever happens to our universities in the future, Washington Square was somehow closer to reality than Cambridge ... .[241]

NOTES

1   *Thomas Wolfe's Letters to His Mother*, ed. John Skally Terry (New York: Charles Scribner's Sons, 1943), pp. xxviii and 6-7. Hereafter this book will be referred to as *Letters to His Mother*.

2   The directness with which he proceeded to Baker on his arrival at Cambridge must be taken as evidence for this, though it should be noted that he indicated journalism as his intended career on his application to the Graduate School at Harvard. See Richard S. Kennedy, "Thomas Wolfe at Harvard, 1920-1923," *Harvard Library Bulletin*, IV, 176.

3   *Letters to His Mother*, p. xxviii. The offer may have been renewed in September. *Ibid.*, p. 6.

4   Koch, founder and director of the Carolina Playmakers, had himself been a student under Baker. Wolfe became a member of Koch's first group in 1918 when he was a junior. The Playmakers staged two one-act plays from his pen, "The Return of Buck Gavin" and "The Third Night." Koch has recorded his impressions of Wolfe at this time in *Carolina Folk Plays; First, Second, and Third Series* (New York: Henry Holt and Company, 1941), pp. 127-31.

5   *Letters to His Mother*, p. 32. This was probably in June of 1921, though he does not mention the fact until July.

6   Kennedy, "Wolfe at Harvard," IV, 180. Wolfe here exaggerates, as he did later, the extent of his reading.

7   *Letters to His Mother*, p. 20, where it is called "The Mountaineers." It may have been given also in the fall of 1920. See *ibid.*, p. 13. But it is more likely that Wolfe, in speaking of the play as having been given "a performance here this Fall," is referring to the previous semester, when the play would have been in rehearsal. Kennedy does not mention an earlier performance than that of January 25, 1921.

8   Kennedy, "Wolfe at Harvard," IV, 188. A preliminary sketch of the play is in *Letters to His Mother*, pp. 14-19. A briefer one will be found *ibid.*, p. 26.

9   *Letters to His Mother*, p. 14. He worked on a revision of it as a one-act play for a public showing, and he hoped that it would be sent on a road trip with other one-act plays. *Ibid.*, p. 21.

10   *Ibid.*, p. 33.

11   *Ibid.*, pp. 32-36. It is only fair to Tom to point out that there was something in this charge of neglect. Though he had notified her on January 25 that his

second-term bills had to be paid by February 10, she obviously had not accommodated him by February 21. *Ibid.*, pp. 20 and 21-22. In March she admonished him for spending money. Kennedy, "Wolfe at Harvard," IV, 188. The correspondence covering the arrangements for summer school has not been published, if it exists, but it would not appear that she wrote him more than once between early June and September 19, 1921. *Letters to His Mother*, p. 34. In her defense it should be pointed out not merely that Tom was difficult but that she had a sick husband, other children who made demands, and was involved in real-estate speculation.

12 The year did, moreover, develop an intimacy between Wolfe and his mentor. Baker had him at his home and took him to see theatrical performances in Boston. *Ibid.*, pp. 38-40.

13 *Ibid.*, p. 25. With better evidence than Professor Terry possessed, Kennedy is able to date this letter "after March or in the spring term of 1922," "Wolfe at Harvard," IV, 179.

14 *Ibid.*, IV, 179. The notebook, however, belongs to 1926. Letter, Kennedy to Cargill, March 23, 1953. Perhaps friction between Wolfe and his fellows can be dated even earlier: "I have suffered a lot by myself on account of my youth in a class of mature men but I've got something to say in my plays. I believe that most of them haven't." *Letters to His Mother*, pp. 36-37. Could Wolfe have kept this distinction to himself?

15 Kennedy, "Wolfe at Harvard," IV, 189.

16 *Letters to His Mother*, p. 25.

17 *Of Time and the River*, pp. 218-73. Before he was offered the position at Northwestern he applied to University College, New York University, for appointment, but got no encouragement. Letter, Nowell to Cargill, February 21, 1953. Nothing remains at New York University to show that this approach was made.

18 Kennedy, "Wolfe at Harvard," IV, 306.

19 *Letters to His Mother*, pp. 38, 41, and 44. Professor Terry thinks the last allusion is to "The Mountains," but the context of the successive letters would make it seem that "Welcome to Our City" was uppermost in Wolfe's mind and the chief object of his labors in 1922-23. He was, however, working on another play off and on (*ibid.*, pp. 41, 45, and 47) and had intended to do three. Note that he had only two in shape to show producers on June 9th. *Ibid.*, p. 55.

20 *Ibid.*, pp. 45 and 47-48; Kennedy, "Wolfe at Harvard," IV, 309-12.

21 *Letters to His Mother*, pp. 45 and 48.

22 *Ibid.*, pp. 48-49 and 54-55.

23 *Ibid.*, p. 48.

24 On August 4 he wrote his mother that he was submitting the play "this week," but on August 31 he tells her that the manuscript had to be retyped, that he is "giving it to the Theatre Guild tomorrow or Monday — Monday, I expect. Tomorrow is the 1st and I believe Labor Day." Between these two dates he had

been with Henry Carlton in Madison, N. H. *Ibid.*, pp. 56-57. Earlier, in the same summer, he visited Harold Duble in Pleasantville, New York. *Ibid.*, pp. 52-56.

25 Letter, Kennedy to Cargill, March 23, 1953. Wolfe had some sort of job after his return from Asheville, soliciting for the Graham Memorial for the University of North Carolina Alumni Association.

26 *Ibid.*, pp. 60-63. The effect of rejection on Wolfe is graphically described in *Of Time and the River*, pp. 360-61. In his letter to Mrs. Roberts of February 10, 1924, Wolfe appears somewhat to exaggerate the length of time the Theatre Guild held his play. See "Writing Is My Life," *The Atlantic*, CLXXVIII (December 1946), 62.

27 Kennedy, "Wolfe at Harvard," IV, 311.

28 Letter, Robert Dow to Oscar Cargill, December 30, 1949. Memorabilia II, 1.

29 *Letters to His Mother*, p. 62. He also mentions the possibility of going to New Hampshire to stay with Henry Carlton until the teaching job materializes.

30 *Ibid.*, p. 62. "Univ." obviously stands for "University." Probably it is the University of North Carolina that owes him money and not Harvard. See note 25 above.

31 *Ibid.*, pp. 65-66.

32 *Ibid.*, p. 67. Wolfe was egocentric without being vain. The evidence is not very conclusive that he ever looked up the reference to himself. He misspells Sayler's name and has the title of his book wrong. But see "Writing Is My Life," *The Atlantic*, CLXXVIII, 63.

33 "Mama, do you realize that it has been over four months since Gene left Harvard and, so far as I can see, he has made no effort yet to get a job. What does he intend to do?" she said angrily. "You know he just can't mope around like this *all* his days! Sooner or later he's got to find some work to do!" *Of Time and the River*, p. 354.

34 Letter I, *The Correspondence of Thomas Wolfe and Homer Andrew Watt* (hereafter referred to as *Wolfe-Watt Correspondence*). *Letters to His Mother*, p. 66.

35 Theodore F. Jones, ed., *New York University, 1832:1932* (New York: New York University Press, 1933), p. 200; *New York University Bulletin: Washington Square College*, XXIV (March 22, 1924), p. 8.

36 Jones, ed., *New York University*, pp. 155-61 and 379. The School of Pedagogy became, of course, the School of Education.

37 *Ibid.*, pp. 188-89, 196-98, and 379-80.

38 When the building housed a shirtwaist factory and was not leased or owned by the University. See Harry Rugoff, *An East Side Epic*, p. 49; Jones, *New York University*, p. 203, n. 6.

39 Jones, ed., *New York University*, p. 384.

40 In setting a master's degree as a minimum requirement for teaching in the early twenties, Washington Square College was establishing a higher standard than

generally prevailed. The author of this essay held positions in two Middle Western colleges with only his bachelor's degree and had plenty of faculty companionship in this status.

41 Dr. Watt edited or collaborated in the following texts: *The Composition of Technical Papers* (1917; rev. ed., 1925); *Ideas and Forms in English and American Literature* (1925; rev. ed., 1930); *Highways in College Composition* (1930); *Outlines of Shakespeare's Plays* (1935; rev. eds., 1938, 1941); *The Literature of England* (1936; rev. eds. 1941, 1947, 1952); *Voices of Liberty* (1941); *New Highways in College Composition* (1943); *Dictionary of English Literature* (1945); *A College Reader* (1948).

42 Letter I, *Wolfe-Watt Correspondence.*

43 Unfinished MS., "Tom Wolfe, Teacher," pp. 2-3.

44 *Letters to His Mother*, p. 66. He could hardly have cut his play to the desired length between January 4 (when he wrote his mother) and January 10 (when he applied to Watt and made this statement).

45 Reproduced by permission of the Harvard Appointment Office. To judge from what has been freshly typed in, the only revisions in this document are under "REMARKS" beginning with "1922-1923" and ending with "book on The American Theatre." The date "June 1922" has been X-ed out in the upper right-hand corner and under "ADDRESS: Present:" what appears to be "67 Hammond Street, Cambridge, Mass." has also been X-ed out. Hence I have supplied these in brackets. See also note 46 below.

46 *Letters to His Mother*, p. 8. It would be interesting to know whether this statement about his height and weight was made in 1922 or 1924. Obviously the entry about his age has been revised; was the rest of the line? There is no typographical evidence in our copy.

47 *Ibid.*, p. 71 (dated March 12, 1924). I have since learned from Edward C. Aswell (conversation, April 2, 1953) that the undertaker told him that Wolfe measured 6 feet, 6 inches at the time of his death and that no coffin in Baltimore would hold his body. I presume this is final, but I have let the other estimates stand to illustrate the biographer's problems in dealing with Wolfe.

48 *Ibid.*, p. ix.

49 "Thomas Wolfe on the Use of Fact in Fiction," *New York Herald Tribune Books* (April 14, 1935), p. 8.

50 "Thomas Wolfe at 35 Is Tired of Being a Legend," *New York Herald Tribune* (November 3, 1935). Clipping, page missing.

51 *From Death to Morning*, p. 134. At nineteen, according to the caption beneath his picture in *Yackety-Yack*, the Carolina senior annual, he was only "6 feet 3 inches." Agatha B. Adams, *Thomas Wolfe: Carolina Student* ("Extension Publications," Vol. XV, No. 2, January) (Chapel Hill: University of North Carolina Library, 1950), p. 7.

52 Adams, *Thomas Wolfe: Carolina Student*, pp. 21-51. For an even longer list, see *ibid.*, p. 7.

53 Letter II, *Wolfe-Watt Correspondence.*

54 *Letters to His Mother,* p. 71. The change in arrangement was probably made orally before Wolfe began to teach, though his first letter to his mother from New York on February 6 does not mention it.

55 Bruce Carpenter is at present an Associate Professor of English, a lecturer on the contemporary theater, a contributing editor to *Theatre Time,* and a very successful author of fiction for adolescents. A native New Yorker, he took his A.B. at Harvard in 1920 and his A.M. the following year when he was in the 47 Workshop with Wolfe. The men never became intimates.

56 Letter III, *Wolfe-Watt Correspondence.*

57 *Letters to His Mother,* p. 68. "Writing Is My Life," *The Atlantic,* CLXVIII, 63. What he means by writing Mrs. Roberts, "I came to New York on a flying trip," is not clear, for there is no other evidence that he came down to New York between January 13, when Dr. Watt wrote him, and when he reported. In 1923-24, the English staff consisted of Professor Watt, Assistant Professor Munn, Messrs. Bopes, Buckham, Carpenter, Clark, Davis, Gibbs, Hawkins, Hoffman, Loggins, McCloskey, MacKellar, Martin, Nichols, Owen, Richards, Schutt, Shoemaker, Varney, Wolfe, and Miss Smith. Professor Nason and Associate Professor Allen, of University College, were each giving a single course late in the afternoon. *New York University Bulletin: Washington Square College,* XXIV (March 22, 1924), 105-10.

58 "Writing Is My Life," *The Atlantic,* CLXVIII, 63.

59 Course reports, Recorder's Office, Washington Square College, May 31 and June 2, 1924. See *Letters to His Mother,* p. 70: "I have about 110 in my three classes, somewhat more than I bargained for, — more than I was promised. This means I have a paper from each one once a week, which must be graded and corrected. That part of teaching is drudgery."

60 *Letters to His Mother,* pp. 68-69.

61 *Of Time and the River,* pp. 428-31.

62 *Letters to His Mother,* pp. 80-81.

63 *Of Time and the River,* pp. 447-54, where the friend is named "Robert Weaver." No fire at the hotel is reported in *The New York Times Index,* 1924-1930, but Professor Terry tells me the fire was extinguished by Wolfe and the manager. The young man involved has since committed suicide. I have confirmation of his death from George W. McCoy of the *Asheville Citizen.* Letter, McCoy to Cargill, June 4, 1953. Terry had the story directly from Wolfe.

64 *Letters to His Mother,* p. 78.

65 *Ibid.,* pp. 72 and 78.

66 *Ibid.,* pp. 75-76.

67 *Ibid.,* p. 79.

68 One does not know how much credence to give to the report of a dozen "mad and sudden journeys" to New England "many times," to Pennsylvania, to Vir-

ginia, and "more than once" up the river toward Albany, ascribed to Eugene in *Of Time and the River*, p. 469. One cannot believe that he had money enough for all these sallies. One piece of reporting, however, seems authentic enough. *Ibid.*, pp. 472-75. Note that the number of trips up the river is set as "eight" on pp. 475 and 476.

69 *Letters to His Mother*, p. 73; see also *Of Time and the River*, p. 441.

70 "Writing Is My Life," *The Atlantic*, CLXXVIII, 63.

71 Adams, *Thomas Wolfe: Carolina Student*, p. 7.

72 Kennedy, "Wolfe at Harvard," IV, 177 ff.

73 Compare what he did (one one-act play and one long play completed) with what Eugene O'Neill probably did in a single year. See *Lost Plays of Eugene O'Neill*, ed. Lawrence Gellert (New York: New Fathoms, 1950), and *Thirst and Other One Act Plays* (New York: privately printed, 1914).

74 *Letters to His Mother*, pp. 70 and 78. Contrast the bold assertion in *Of Time and the River* (p. 443): "but he was a good teacher, . . . he had paid his way . . . ."

75 *Of Time and the River*, pp. 477-78.

76 See Letter, Dow to Cargill, December 30, 1949. ". . . I saw Tom several times sometime in the following winter. . . . Once at the Albert Hotel . . . we had a few drinks. . . . Tom was being very man about town with sexy remarks (as we said in the slang of those days) and innuendoes about the girl at the cigar counter in the hotel. I remember that I was somewhat surprised because Tom hadn't seemed like that at Cambridge and because it all seemed very like the travelling salesmen who are such hot numbers in a country hotel. Or used to be . . . ." Just previously Wolfe had written, "Moral turpitude on the physical basis does not offend me deeply." "Writing Is My Life," *The Atlantic*, CLXXVIII, 62.

77 *Of Time and the River*, pp. 478-79. It should be observed that this is a generalized statement and that the girls in no one class are alluded to. At times Wolfe was very conscious of his anti-Semitism and its injustice. He discussed it and asked what he could do about it with Professor Harry Charipper of the Biology Department and with Abraham I. Katsh, then a student and now Professor of Hebrew Culture and Education, in the School of Education, New York University. Conversations with Pollock, May 1953. See also Volkening, Memorabilia II, 2.

78 *Of Time and the River*, pp. 440 ff. What elements are fictional and what are real in this portrait it is impossible to say.

79 *Ibid.*, pp. 440-41.

80 The collection may have been *Adventures in Essay Reading*, ed. Department of Rhetoric and Journalism of the University of Michigan (New York: Harcourt, Brace and Company, 1923), a moderately good collection of essays but with too many academics among the authors.

81 *Of Time and the River*, p. 444.

82 *Ibid.*, pp. 455-68.

83 "The Reviewing Stand," *Parkchester Press-Review,* November 29, 1945, p. 10, col. 1. Gerald Doyle was in English 35, September 1929-February 1930, the last class Wolfe taught. It met Thursday evenings from 8 to 9:45 P.M. Doyle received a B along with Nathan Shackman. These were the highest grades in the course.

84 "I Knew Thomas Wolfe," *Fact Digest,* V (March 1938), 15-16. Ehrsam was in English 35-36, September-June 1927-28. Course Reports, February 1 and May 29, 1928, Recorder's Office, Washington Square College.

85 Letters, B. W. Kofsky to Pollock, March 10, 1950; A. G. Doyle to Cargill, *ca.* December 1949. Wolfe extended his reading into the Composition classes, a practice that had some vogue in the twenties. It also protected him from questioning to some extent.

86 Letter, C. R. Smith to Pollock, December 12, 1949. Miss Smith was in Education 110.3-4, Ideas and Forms in English and American Literature, September-June 1925-26, and received the only A in the course. Course Report, June 1, 1926, Recorder's Office, Washington Square College.

87 Letter, A. S. Pegues to Pollock, February 20, 1950. Pegues, who was in the Department of English Education, had a kind of oversight of the courses in English given for his department by Washington Square College, so that his interest in Wolfe's performance was a natural one. There was, and is, no "visitation" in Washington Square College classes.

88 Course Reports, May 31 and June 2, 1924, and February 1, 3, 5, and 6, 1930, Recorder's Office, Washington Square College. Two of the latter reports are for the College of Fine Arts but were filed with the Washington Square College recorder. Commenting to Russell Krauss who took the section over from him on giving 9 F's and 14 D's in one section, Wolfe remarks, "Even so, I was probably generous."

89 "Writing Is My Life," *The Atlantic,* CLXXVIII, 64.

90 *Letters to His Mother,* p. 85.

91 Ehrsam, "I Knew Thomas Wolfe," p. 16.

92 Unpublished paper by Daniel Lawrence. See also Leon Edel, *Henry James: The Untried Years* (Philadelphia: J. B. Lippincott Company, 1953), p. 40.

93 *Letters to His Mother,* p. 81.

94 John Terry, Tom's best friend, gratified the author a number of years ago by telling him that Wolfe said he liked him very much. Wolfe was interested in baseball, and the author had had a very, very brief experience as a sports writer with the Worcester *Telegram-Gazette,* which Wolfe somehow got an exaggerated notion of. Miss Nowell has helped me to locate the childbirth episode in the spring of 1928; I remembered the twilight and had placed it in the winter.

95 "Writing Is My Life," *The Atlantic,* CLXXVIII, 63.

96 *The Web and the Rock,* p. 389.

97 *Of Time and the River,* p. 422.

NOTES

98 *You Can't Go Home Again*, p. 16.

99 *Of Time and the River*, p. 420.

100 The professor satirized has edited several controversial books in which the treatment of sex is a moot point. His sane handling of the topic in his Introductions clears him of the charge of "obscene puritanism." Probably the criticism which most irritated Wolfe was that he lacked power to give his creative work form — the very criticism that Baker had made of it.

101 A legend exists at Washington Square that *Of Time and the River* once contained an even more violent caricature of Professor Watt, who was uniformly kind to Wolfe and that Maxwell Perkins made him take it out. I have not been able to verify this in the smallest way and think it apocryphal. There is a passage in MS. 46 AM-7 (65), Box 1, in the Houghton Library satirizing "Associate Professor Alonzo Spurgeon" but this does not appear to be a portrait of Dr. Watt. Letter, William A. Jackson to Cargill, March 13, 1953.

102 Letters, B. W. Kofsky to Pollock, March 10, 1950; A. G. Doyle to Cargill, *ca.* December 1949.

103 Mrs. Bernstein. See the chapter "Glory Deferred" in *The Web and the Rock*.

104 See "Replacing Thomas Wolfe," Memorabilia II, 4.

105 See Letter, James B. Munn to Watt, September 20, 1925.

106 Some have held that the treatment of Wolfe's colleagues in his novels should not be taken too literally. This is the view of Desmond Powell, editor of the *Arizona Quarterly*, who was once a teacher with Wolfe in Washington Square College: "He was especially annoyed by those who sought to identify characters and incidents in his stories with real persons and events. *Once when remarking on the pleasant personal relationships he had had in New York University* [italics ours] he added, 'I don't suppose I shall ever be able to say anything about academics that won't be taken as a criticism of my former colleagues. Nevertheless there are things I feel I must say.' He did not have time to express them all in his books. He believed, for example, that there was in the academic atmosphere something inimical to writing; he thought that there was considerable confusion about the relations of undergraduate teaching to graduate scholarship; he suggested that college teachers were often men of limited understanding because they were men of narrow experience; he commented upon the fact that many academics are never out of the schoolroom from the age of five or six until the day of their death or retirement; he looked with approval on George Lincoln Burr's proposal that every student of the humanities be required to earn his living for a year with his hands before being admitted to the graduate school. Such ideas as these he wished to embody in his work; but he feared that however he embodied them, someone would take it as a personal attack." "Of Thomas Wolfe," *Arizona Quarterly*, I, 29.

107 *The Web and the Rock*, p. 457. Italics mine.

108 *Of Time and the River*, p. 442.

109 *Letters to His Mother*, p. 74.

74

110 *Ibid.*, pp. 82-84.

111 *Of Time and the River*, pp. 500-96. Olin Dows is said by Terry to be represented as Joel Pierce in the novel.

112 *Letters to His Mother*, pp. 81-82. It does not appear that Wolfe added a third act to the play this year. See letter to Dr. Watt, January 15, 1925, in which he says the prologue and *two acts* of his play were stolen in Paris.

113 *Of Time and the River*, pp. 544-49. One is to infer that he read the portion he had done. In passing, note the self-criticism in the novel of the play — it is "a young man's play" made up of the "good and bad" and marked by his idolatries: "Shakespeare, Chekhov, Shaw, Rostand, the Bible." It is a "groping and uncertain play" yet of course has elements of greatness.

114 "Writing Is My Life," *The Atlantic*, CLXXVIII, 64.

115 "Writing Is My Life," *The Atlantic* (January 1947), CLXXIX, 39. See also *Letters to His Mother*, p. 86. The intermediary was Ann Macdonald, a reader and translator at the Neighborhood Playhouse. Letter, Nowell to Cargill, February 21, 1953.

116 *Letters to His Mother*, p. 73. It is in this letter that he mentions for the first time "the great novel" that waits to be written. Wolfe overestimated what would be due him. See *ibid.*, p. 90.

117 *Ibid.*, pp. 85-86.

118 *Ibid.*, p. 78.

119 *Ibid.*, p. 93.

120 *Ibid.*, p. 92.

121 *Ibid.*, pp. 98-103. Letter to Dr. Watt, January 15, 1925.

122 *Ibid.*, pp. 103-7. *Of Time and the River*, pp. 680-794 and 886. Kennedy tells me that "Starwick's" homosexuality does not figure in the letters that Wolfe wrote "Ann" after the breakup. Letter, Kennedy to Cargill, March 23, 1953.

123 *Of Time and the River*, pp. 797-849 and 870-77. He went from Orléans to Tours then back to Orléans according to the novel. But it was in Tours he met the Countess. *Letters to His Mother*, p. 108; or was it? See Letter VII, *Wolfe-Watt Correspondence*.

124 Letter IV, *Wolfe-Watt Correspondence*. Kennedy writes (March 23, 1953) ". . . a fragment of a note to Watt [in the Harvard Library] seems to indicate that Wolfe had received the offer from Watt in 1924-1925, but never replied. The fragment is undated, but he begins by saying he accepts the offer of an instructorship in the Feb.-Sept. term."

125 Letter V, *Wolfe-Watt Correspondence*.

126 Letter IV, *Wolfe-Watt Correspondence*. Also a letter of February 5, 1925, from Dr. Watt to Dean John R. Turner recommending the appointment of Terry: "I feel that under the circumstances we have done very well to appoint him. It is difficult, as you can understand, to secure a satisfactory instructor on a few days'

notice in the middle of the year. I did the best I could under the circumstances and conferred definitely with several candidates."

127 Terry docket, Department of English Office, Washington Square College. Also letter, Maxwell Perkins to H. A. Watt, January 16, 1940. John Terry's death occurred in the week beginning June 28, 1953.

128 Letter VI, *Wolfe-Watt Correspondence.* There is no record of Wolfe having an argument with the Negro elevator men; probably what Watt refers to is the fact that Wolfe once walked down seven floors rather than be carried by a specific operator. See Leah R. Middlebrook, "Reminiscences of Tom Wolfe," *American Mercury,* LXIII (November 1946), 545.

129 Letter VIII, *Wolfe-Watt Correspondence.*

130 *Letters to His Mother,* p. 109. The copyist of Wolfe's letters (sometimes very difficult to read) transcribed the name as "Professor Arnold." Mrs. Koch tells Elizabeth Nowell that "the professor Tom visited in St. Raphael was Professor D. D. Carroll of the University of North Carolina." Letter, Nowell to Pollock, February 6, 1950, postscript. Actually he did not even visit the Carrolls; they had left St. Raphael by the time he had raised money enough to get there. Letter, Kennedy to Cargill, March 22, 1953.

131 His statement in his letter of that date to his mother mentioning the New York University offer and remarking, "I shall probably be back there" (*Letters to His Mother,* p. 111), indicates that he had not yet reached a conclusion in his own mind.

132 Letter VII, *Wolfe-Watt Correspondence.*

133 It isn't very clear what this chance was. Did he hope to persuade his mother, who had recently trebled her capital, to support him longer? Or did he hope to sell the account of his travels on which he had been working?

134 *Letters to His Mother,* pp. 72 and 78.

135 *Of Time and the River,* pp. 130 ff., 167 ff., and 282 ff.

136 Letter IX, *Wolfe-Watt Correspondence.* This letter may help explain why Wolfe was known among the irreverent in the department as "Dr. Watt's vicarious catharsis." Letter, Helen H. Gude to Cargill, December 31, 1952.

137 Letter X, *Wolfe-Watt Correspondence.*

138 Letter XI, *Wolfe-Watt Correspondence.* The "D's" and "M's" in the program are for sections of predental and premedical students — a distinction kept for only a short while.

139 "Writing Is My Life," *The Atlantic,* CLXXVIII, 65.

140 *Of Time and the River,* pp. 661-80 ("picked out at random from the ferment of ten thousand pages, and a million words").

141 *Letters to His Mother,* pp. 124 and 126-27. Note that the principal character of *Mannerhouse* is "Eugene," named in anticipation of "Eugene Gant."

142 In "Faust and Helen," *Of Time and the River*, pp. 907-12, there is a fictional treatment of such an experience. Professor Waldo Buckham of the School of Commerce, formerly a member of the Department of English of the College, remembers Wolfe walking about the office on his return, ecstatically exclaiming, "I'm in love! I'm in love!" Conversation with Cargill, February 1953.

143 This account of Mrs. Bernstein is drawn from the jacket blurbs on her novels and from mutual friends in the theatrical world and elsewhere. There are unpublished and unavailable letters in the Harvard Library between the pair.

144 Compare *An Actor's Daughter* (New York: Alfred A. Knopf, 1941), pp. 16-18, and *Look Homeward, Angel*, pp. 27, 66, etc.

145 See *An Actor's Daughter*, p. 43: "Maybe if I had not been so fond of food the whole color of my life would have been different." Wolfe's case hardly needs documentation.

146 "I came here almost two months ago . . . suffering from a bad attack of heartbreak." Wolfe from St. Raphael to his mother, May 26, 1925. *Letters to His Mother*, p. 113.

147 Tom during this period responded very little to pretty girls of his own age. There were several at different times in the Department of English at Washington Square during his stay. One of these, who does herself scant justice in delineation, has the following interesting estimate of him: ". . . I never did know Tom Wolfe, except to say hello to casually. I was the conventional, moderately pretty, moderately well-suited girl — the type that never would interest him. His manner toward me, as towards others of this type, was always so polite that it seemed strained.

"I remember that I met him first at the Henry Volkenings. He had just come back from Europe, and having heard of him as 'Dr. Watt's vicarious catharsis' . . . I expected something robust from him. What I got was a query as to how long I'd been in New York and what I thought of the skyline. He wasn't having a quiet brand of fun either, I felt — he was ill at ease and disinterested. Our subsequent brief conversations were carried on at the same sparkling level.

"The only time he ever changed from his almost old-fashioned courtesy was a night at the James Thurbers, when I met him after we'd both been out of the department for some years. We had a little polite chit-chat. After some hours and some highballs, the talk turned to women and I made some casual remark in their defense. He called me a bitch — said all women were bitches. I'd always felt about him that under the veneer of politeness there was a deep hatred of all women except a few. That was the evening he burst into tears and sobbed, 'I've never had a bank account. God damn it, I've never had a bank account.' . . ." Letter, Helen Howard Gude to Cargill, December 31, 1952.

148 Course Reports (undated, with one exception, March 13) for February 1926 and for May 22, 24, and June 1 and 19, Washington Square College. It looks as if the sections set up for Monday, Wednesday, and Friday, 2:00-3:00 and 5:00-6:00, did not fill, and Wolfe was given, in addition to his Monday, Wednesday, and Friday, 3:00-4:00, section of English 1-2 and his Thursday, 4:15-6:00, section of English 110.3-4, a section of English 1 meeting Tuesday and Thursday, 6:30-7:50; the

literature section, English 110.3-4, appears to have been shifted to Saturday morning, 9:15-11:00; the second semester, in addition to continuing his other sections, Wolfe got a section of English 2 on Monday, Wednesday, and Friday from 5 to 6 P.M. Procedures have changed, and it is somewhat difficult to interpret the records.

149 Letter, James B. Munn to Cargill, October 5, 1949. The best reason for thinking this letter refers to 1925-26 is that Munn speaks of Wolfe teaching in the evening, which Wolfe did not do in the February-September 1924 session. On the other hand, Munn remembers the department as being in "the big faculty room" (where it was in 1924) but adds in parentheses with a question mark "806?"; the office number in the Main Building was 206. It is curious that Munn remembers the Albert as on Eighth Street, for Wolfe lived on Eighth Street the next time he was at the College, 1927-28. Writing all night came later, too. See below, note 167.

150 Carlton docket, Department of English, Washington Square College. George Baker and Will D. Howe of Scribner's wrote letters endorsing Carlton. Carlton's play was tried out in New York at the Morosco in December, 1926. Note, Watt to Carlton, December 2, 1926. With William Ford Manley, another 47 Workshop man who was hired by Munn and joined the staff the next year, Carlton began writing plays for the radio. They were so successful that they resigned in 1928. Letter, Carlton to Watt, February 10, 1928. I remember the pair as utter madcaps.

151 *Letters to His Mother*, pp. 123-24.

152 *Ibid.*, pp. 131 and 132. See also *The Story of a Novel*. Mrs. Bernstein, however, says Wolfe told her that he began the novel at Ilkley and finished outlining it there, that he continued the book in London. See Pamela H. Johnson, *Hungry Gulliver, an English Critical Appraisal* (New York: Charles Scribner's Sons, 1948), p. 2. n. 2. This author locates the London rooming house in Horseferry Road, Westminster, rather than in Chelsea. Note that in a letter to Mrs. Roberts on July 19, 1926, from Bath, Wolfe has begun a novel that he thinks of calling *The Building of a Wall*, "Writing Is My Life," *The Atlantic*, CLXXVIII, 66.

153 John Donne, "A Valediction of My Name, in the Window," *Poems of John Donne* (London: Routledge, The Muses Library, 2 vols., n.d.) I, 26, st. v.

154 *Letters to His Mother*, p. 75.

155 *Ibid.*, pp. 46-47. March 31, 1923, when he was still at Harvard.

156 *The Magic Curtain* (New York: E. P. Dutton and Company, 1951), p. 159.

157 *You Can't Go Home Again*, pp. 432-36 and 460-82.

158 *Ibid.*, pp. 240 ff.

159 *Letters to His Mother*, pp. 131, 133 and 136.

160 *Of Time and the River*, pp. 644-52.

161 *Letters to His Mother*, pp. 137 and 138.

162 *Ibid.*, p. 132.

163 Letter XII, *Wolfe-Watt Correspondence*. Professor Watt had corrected the date on this from 1926 to 1927.

164 *Letters to His Mother*, p. 138.

165 *Ibid.*, p. 141.

166 *Ibid.*, p. 138.

167 *Ibid.*, p. 138. Wolfe merely mentions Eighth Street; the precise address is in the Wolfe docket, Dean's Office. Letter, Weston to Nowell, February 16, 1951. The building has been completely remodeled; shops now occupy the lower floor, which extends out to the sidewalk. Assistant Professor Boris Gamzue furnishes some details of Wolfe's existence at this time:

"My next recollection is of visits to his loft residence on Eighth Street, east of University Place [this is incorrect], on the north side of the street. He was the only inhabitant of the building after five or six o'clock; the lower floors housed light manufacturing firms. The impression I have of this loft is of an enormous room where he could comfortably take his enormous strides. He had recently been given the idea of writing in ledgers, and the floor was piled with ledgers he had filled.

"My habit was to work until about midnight. Occasionally I would drop in on Tom after work and we would go out for a light bite and a hot rum poncino in one of the many Village places that sold the cheap prohibition drink (15 or 20 cents). Then Tom would go to work, for he wrote chiefly throughout the night.

"I must have visited him there also in the daytime, for it was there he first introduced me to Aline Bernstein, who was actively associated with the Neighborhood Playhouse. I understood, though I don't know how I knew it, that she was seeing Tom through financially, at least to the extent of paying the rent on the loft.

"During this period, I went uptown to dinner with Tom at least once. I remember calling for him at the loft, then going with him to the Harvard Club, where he got his mail and took baths (there was no bath in the loft building). He also kept a bottle of prohibition whiskey in a locker at the Harvard Club. After a drink or two of that whiskey, we went to a midtown restaurant. Tom devoured an enormous pompano for dinner.

". . . Tom had a play under consideration by the Neighborhood Playhouse. He was getting discouraged at their delay in making up their minds about it. Apparently by spring they either rejected it or he had decided to withdraw it, for he asked me if I'd mind keeping the manuscript for him over the summer while he went abroad. I agreed to do it, but he never got around to giving me the manuscript. . . .

"I remember seeing him later at an apartment he had in the west Village. On one occasion, Aline Bernstein was there and served tea. I think the boy who had typed Tom's manuscript was also present then. Tom seemed very grateful to him . . . ." Letter, Gamzue to Cargill, February 19, 1953.

168 Letter XIII, *Wolfe-Watt Correspondence*.

169 Letter XIV, *Wolfe-Watt Correspondence*.

170 *Letters to His Mother*, pp. 141 and 145; "Writing Is My Life," *The Atlantic*, CLXXVIII, 66.

171 *Letters to His Mother*, pp. 142, 145. See also Letters XV and XVI, *Wolfe-Watt Correspondence*, which indicate that part of the arrangements were oral, though a letter sent Wolfe on June 2 or 3 is missing. See *Letters to His Mother*, p. 142, and Letter XVIII, *Wolfe-Watt Correspondence*.

172 See Letter XVIII, *Wolfe-Watt Correspondence*.

173 *Editor to Author: The Letters of Maxwell E. Perkins* (New York: Charles Scribner's Sons, 1950), pp. 98 and 122. Perkins took the position that the beliefs Wolfe gave Eugene were Wolfe's in 1934 and 1935 and not Eugene's in the time of the book.

174 *Ibid.*, pp. 226-27, 278, and 279. Perkins states that political divergence between him and Tom was of no consequence.

175 Letter XVII, *Wolfe-Watt Correspondence*.

176 Letter XIX, *Wolfe-Watt Correspondence*.

177 Course Reports, January 27, 28, one undated, and February 1, 1928, Recorder's Office, Washington Square College.

178 Course Reports, May 18, 26, 29, and one undated, 1928, Recorder's Office, Washington Square College.

179 *Letters to His Mother*, pp. 151, 162. The actual address was discovered by Elizabeth Nowell on a letter from Tom Smith, of Boni and Liveright, dealing with *Look Homeward, Angel*. Nowell to Jean Weston, February 21, 1951. For a description of this place by Wolfe himself, see *You Can't Go Home Again*, pp. 3-4. But the house is west of Fourth Street and removed from the hospital; it is a mid-nineteenth-century brick house with a brownstone stoop — the best residence Wolfe had in New York.

180 "Thomas Wolfe," *Harvard Library Bulletin*, I (Autumn 1947), 277.

181 "Thomas Wolfe: Penance No More," Memorabilia, II, 2.

182 Letter, Kennedy to Cargill, March 23, 1953; also *Letters to His Mother*, p. 150. I cannot discover who this former student was. Tradition says that he was "Abe Jones," whom I have not been able to locate.

183 Letter, James B. Munn to Cargill, October 5, 1949. Munn remembers the title of the manuscript when he read it as *Ah, God* or what appears to be that. He had remembered the title perfectly in 1947 (Letter, Munn to Jack Mandell, April 11, 1947). I have changed the material in the parenthesis. Prior to this, Wolfe had called the book *Alone, Alone*. See "Writing Is My Life," *The Atlantic*, CLXXIX, 39.

184 *Letters to His Mother*, p. 156.

185 "Writing Is My Life," *The Atlantic*, CLXXIX, 40.

186 Letter, James B. Munn to Cargill, October 5, 1949.

187 *The Web and the Rock*, p. 488.

188 *Ibid.*, pp. 488-515.

189 *Ibid.*, p. 517. And following quotation.

190 *The Web and the Rock*, pp. 524 ff.; *You Can't Go Home Again*, pp. 15-16.

191 Perkins, *Editor to Author*, p. 60; "Wolfe and Perkins," *The Saturday Review of Literature*, XXXIV (August 11, 1951), 22. Several, rather than "numerous," publishers saw the manuscript. One publisher, who saw it before Wolfe turned it over to Mrs. Boyd, was discouraged by the length of it. *Letters to His Mother*, pp. 159, 161.

192 *The Web and the Rock*, pp. 520-36. "Mrs. Boyd says that Ernest Boyd never read the manuscript." Letter, Kennedy to Cargill, March 23, 1953.

193 *Letters to His Mother*, p. 160; Perkins, *Editor to Author*, p. 60.

194 Le Gette Blythe, "The Thomas Wolfe I Knew," *The Saturday Review of Literature*, XXVIII (August 25, 1945), p. 19; Adams, *Thomas Wolfe: Carolina Student*, pp. 36-37.

195 Russell Krauss, "Replacing Tom Wolfe," Memorabilia, II, 4.

196 If this analysis seems improbable, it follows that of the last third of *The Web and the Rock*. See especially pp. 374 and 539. It is augmented, of course, by my acquaintance with the people at the College — not all alike — who went to Wolfe's rooms. Sherwood Anderson once told me a terrible story of Wolfe drunk and raging against Mrs. Bernstein in this vein.

197 *Ibid.*, pp. 462 and 463. Note Wolfe's analysis of Mrs. Jack's success and his growing *dislike for the theater,* especially.

198 "Tom told me that once he woke up to find himself in the gutter of West 42nd St., surrounded by the Salvation Army, who were using him as the text of a sermon on the evils of drink." Letter, William Tindall to Cargill, January 3, 1950. Terry thinks that Wolfe was spoofing Tindall. Conceding that Wolfe drank inordinately, he contends that Wolfe, however drunk, remained always on his feet. Letter, Terry to Cargill, February 19, 1953.

199 *The Web and the Rock*, p. 458.

200 Letter, William Tindall to Cargill, January 3, 1950.

201 *The Web and the Rock*, p. 604. Generally readers have reacted with natural distaste against the long scenes of mutual vituperation in this book and have wondered about Wolfe's lack of reticence. It seems to me that this long exposition of the quarrel was intended as an added chapter in the natural history of love and, without reference to its autobiographic significance, has value for its attempted study of the phases in the growth of disaffection. Much of it, surely, is imagined and fiction.

202 Letter XX, *Wolfe-Watt Correspondence.* Watt made an oral offer at the end of March to Wolfe of a position if he would return in September 1928. *Letters to His Mother*, p. 157.

81

203 J. Walter Thompson Company offered Wolfe a job writing advertising copy, but he had to promise to stay three years, beginning in October 1928, and he was unwilling to do this. *Letters to His Mother*, p. 159.

204 *You Can't Go Home Again*, p. 5; *Letters to His Mother*, pp. 165-75.

205 "Writing Is My Life," *The Atlantic*, CLXXIX, 41; *Letters to His Mother*, p. 173. Chapters 47, "A Visit to the Fair," and 48, "The Hospital," in *The Web and the Rock* give a fictionalized version of the brawl at the Munich beer festival.

206 *Letters to His Mother*, p. 175; "Writing Is My Life," *The Atlantic*, CLXXIX, 41.

207 "Writing Is My Life," *The Atlantic*, CLXXIX, 47.

208 "Thomas Wolfe," *Harvard Library Bulletin* I (Autumn 1947), 270-71. For justification of the comparison to Shelley, see the Frontispiece to this volume.

209 "Writing Is My Life," *The Atlantic*, CLXXIX, 43-44.

210 *Ibid.*, p. 44.

211 There is no documentary proof of this, beyond the implication in Wolfe's letter to Mrs. Roberts on January 12, 1929, "I shall write . . . telling you about my N.Y.U. plans" ("Writing Is My Life," *The Atlantic*, CLXXIX, 44), but I was working very closely with Dr. Watt on a rhetoric at that time and this is my recollection.

212 *Ibid.*, p. 43. The house on Fifteenth Street is in a shabby neighborhood. It is a four-story, brownstone building, with a high white-domed entrance, with stairs up from the sidewalk. In the basement is "Ben's Lunch."

213 Memorandum to Professors Watt and Oglesby, January 28, 1929.

214 Letter, Watt to Bossange, January 31, 1929. Actually the job was in the pristine Division of Architecture, at 9-11 East Thirty-seventh Street, one of the casualties of the depression.

215 Bossange to Watt, February 4, 1929.

216 The Mr. Beals of this letter is Ralph Beals, then an instructor in the Department of English, but now chief librarian of the New York Public Library. He edited an anthology of descriptive and narrative pieces with Tom's friend, John Terry, and another instructor, Mary Barnicle.

217 Letter, Munn to Cargill, October 5, 1949; Letter, Munn to "Jack" Mandel, April 11, 1947. Mr. Mandel is at present chairman of the Department of Biology and General Science of the DeWitt Clinton High School, New York City.

218 James Mandel, "Thomas Wolfe, a Reminiscence," Memorabilia, I, 3.

219 *Letters to His Mother*, p. 176.

220 *Ibid.*, pp. 181-84.

221 Letter, Watt to Munn, April 11, 1929.

222 Letter, Watt to Bossange, May 18, 1929.

223 Letter, Bossange to Watt, May 20, 1929.

224 *Letters to His Mother*, p. 179. The offer appears to have been an oral one, for no documents exist.

225 Course Reports, February 5 and 6, 1930, Recorder's Office, Washington Square College.

226 *Scribner's Magazine* (August 1929) pp. 205-10; there was also a portrait of Tom and a sketch of him in the "Behind the Scenes" section, pp. 29 and 31.

227 James Mandel, "Thomas Wolfe, A Reminiscence," Memorabilia, I, 3.

228 *Letters to His Mother*, pp. 189 and 190.

229 *You Can't Go Home Again*, pp. 148-332.

230 Letters, Nowell to Cargill, February 21, 1953, and Kennedy to Cargill, March 23, 1953. The story "Eugene" in Mrs. Bernstein's *Three Blue Suits* indicates that Eugene did not tell his friend that he was an applicant for a fellowship and was leaving her and going abroad. This may have been another factor in the complex issues of the severed relationship.

231 Struthers Burt, "Wolfe and Perkins," *The Saturday Review of Literature*, XXXIV (August 11, 1951), 23. Burt believes Wolfe's treatment killed Perkins and has produced a letter from one of Perkins' daughters to prove the fact (*ibid.*, p. 25) when readers of *The Saturday Review* attacked him. Wolfe's state was induced by his break with Scribner's over the settlement of a libel suit and the bill for corrections on *Of Time and the River*.

232 *Letters to His Mother*, p. 193. Actually these advances were stopped when Wolfe began to receive moneys from the Guggenheim award.

233 This was a favorite story of Dr. Watt, who had it from Mrs. Watt, a member of the club. I heard him tell it many times.

234 Letter XXI, *Wolfe-Watt Correspondence*. The May lecture was not given.

235 Letter, William Tindall to Cargill, January 3, 1950. Actually Tindall gave his lecture in the adult education division on Friday, October 17, 1930, in a course entitled "What the Modern Writers Are Doing." See *New York University Bulletin*, XXX (September 6, 1930), p. 15.

236 Russell Krauss, "Replacing Tom Wolfe," Memorabilia, II, 4. Krauss is now Associate Professor of English at New Jersey State Teachers College, Montclair, New Jersey.

237 Carbon, Wolfe Docket, Department of English Office. Reprinted by arrangement with the Guggenheim Foundation.

238 Letter, Henry Allen Moe to Dr. Watt, July 30, 1941.

239 Letters XXI and XXII, *Wolfe-Watt Correspondence*.

240 Letter I, Supplement, *Wolfe-Watt Correspondence*.

241 Letter II, Supplement, *Wolfe-Watt Correspondence*.
 The Richmond meeting of the Modern Language Association in December 1936 provided an odd finale to Wolfe's connection with New York University, for there he encountered, quite by chance, both Tindall, who had helped to sell

Look Homeward, Angel, and Dr. Watt. Tindall writes, "While standing with Professor Wright in the lobby of the Jefferson Hotel, I was astonished to see Tom Wolfe striding through towing a young lad of about 18. I went up to Tom and said, 'Why, Tom, I'm glad to see you.' He looked down at me from his eminence and said, 'Tindall.' I asked: 'What are you doing here?' He replied, 'None of your business,' and dashed with the lad into the elevator. That was the last time I saw Wolfe. . . . Wolfe seems to have been well oiled." Letter, Tindall to Cargill, January 3, 1950.

"Tom was not so oiled that he failed to remember this incident. He told me about it, and also mentioned his deep dislike for Tindall. Tom also told me that the youth he was with was his nephew from Anderson, South Carolina." Letter, Terry to Cargill, February 19, 1953.

Dr. William Watt of Lafayette College, who accompanied his father to the meeting, writes me (January 27, 1953): "I remember the Richmond encounter vividly. To say that Wolfe was 'a little drunk' is verily, litotes; he was reeling. And I distinctly remember a pint bottle protruding from his hip pocket. I am sure that he was not attending the meetings of the MLA out of any nostalgic recollections of the scholar's life; but whether he came to the hotel, knowing that the convention was in town, on the chance that he might bump into some of his old colleagues, or whether, as seems more likely, he reeled into the midst of a piece of his past entirely by accident — I don't know. I do know that he literally threw his big arms around my father's neck and affectionately greeted him as 'Homer.' I remember this clearly because I asked Dad if Wolfe had ever called him 'Homer' before, and he said no. I remember being introduced and having most of the juice squeezed out of my own hand by Wolfe's right ham. . . . And I remember somebody in the department (perhaps it was Tindall) coming up and saying, 'Hello, Tom,' and being coldly rebuffed. . . . I am sure the meeting did not extend beyond the brief encounter in the hotel lobby (Tom, I think, had to make a train Southward) and that I was there all the time . . . ."

After this entire book was in page proof a letter was received from Charles F. Bopes, an instructor in the College in Wolfe's time. A Southerner, Bopes became friendly with Wolfe; Tom met Bopes's mother at an invitation performance of *Desire Under the Elms* and was invited to the Bopes home where he went several times and on special occasions. Letter, Bopes to Cargill, August 31, 1953. This suggests that Wolfe may have enjoyed a limited social life during the Washington Square period that did not get into his books or letters.

II · MEMORABILIA

MEMORABILIA

1 · HIS STUDENTS REMEMBER

"DRUNK WITH WORDS"

A. GERALD DOYLE[1]

Press-Review
East Bronx — Parkchester
84 Hugh J. Grant Circle
New York 60, N. Y.

Mr. Oscar Cargill,
Chairman, Department of English,
NYU, Washington Sq. College,
Washington Square, New York 3, N. Y.

Dear Mr. Cargill:

I am extremely interested in your letter of December 27, in which you ask for some information for possible use in your introduction to the correspondence of Thomas Wolfe.

The writer it was who wrote the brief squib in his "Reviewing Stand" column in the November 29, 1945 issue of the Press-Review. I am not sure just when Wolfe was my instructor — I know it was when his great "Look Homeward Angel" was published, if that will give you the time reference. He was my instructor in a sophomore night English class in Washington Square College (or possibly the

---

[1] A. Gerald Doyle, who is today columnist and editorial writer for the East Bronx–Parkchester *Press-Review,* was in Wolfe's English 35 (Types of Literature) class, meeting on Thursdays from 8 to 9:45 P.M. from September 1929 to January 1930.

School of Commerce, Accounts and Finance, I attended both, and can't for the life of me straighten out my chronology).

My most vivid impression of the man was his busting into class one night, clutching a smashed hat to one side of his bosom and a brightly jacketed copy of his new book over his heaving heart. He was out of the world and a Gant, for fair. (Only one or two members of the class of about 30 ever bothered to have him autograph a copy of the novel.)

Another time we were reading aloud, a stanza per pupil from "St. Agnes' Eve," and it was my lot to read the lovely one about the "silver snarling trumpet 'gan to chide." I sensed the beauty of the words and the clangor of the words cued by the opening door, but I was too timid to "read with expression." He shook his head impatiently and re-read the stanza as it should be read, with hot and cadenced vigor. It was a lasting lesson in poetry.

Wolfe was by long odds the most interesting instructor I ever had at NYU. The impact of the man was terrific. He often appeared to be bored with the prosiness of the syllabus, and bored with the members of the class, too. But he made the great writers live when they challenged his imagination.

I found at that time that I was enchanted with the man's other-worldiness. He seemed fey, yet tremendously robust. At one time he was the faun — his small head, delicately poised on that great frame always had me looking for foxy pointed ears. Next he was the epitome of what I then considered your Elizabethan toss-pot should be, storming and spuming (literally), drunk with words and thoughts and electric with living.

In class conversation he sometimes left no doubt that *Look Homeward Angel* was autobiographic, even to the point of quoting words which I found later in the book in which one of the boys asked for a piece of paper "before I bust you in the eye."

There never was any indication that I found of Wolfe's infection with anti-Semitism. He might have been anti-night school students, or anti-New York, but I can recall no instance of any overt anti-

Semitism. It's significant that some of his passages in his novels might be construed as anti-Semitic by those who try too hard to find that ugly thing. But I believe he wasn't anti-Semitic any more than Dickens was when he wrote of the Jews as a part of the scene in England. And it has been my experience that most of the people I know who are highest in praise of Wolfe are Jewish, which doesn't necessarily mean that he or they were conscious of any bent in this direction.

A large proportion of my class under Wolfe was composed of Jewish young men and women. I think that if there had been any evidence of bigotry it should have aroused at least fleeting comment. This I never heard. I think that Wolfe was far too great of stature to stoop to anti-Semitism. Others may have proof of it. You have not mentioned it without reason. But I didn't know of it then, and I don't know of it now.

You are at fullest liberty to quote from my 1945 squib, if you wish, or anything in this letter, although there's scant material.

I have read everything of Wolfe's except the work published by his mother. I shall be keen upon seeing this new one you have in process. You'll do me a favor by placing my order in advance of publication.

> Very truly yours,
>
> A. Gerald Doyle

"OVERLOADED BLACK BRIEFCASE"

BERNARD W. KOFSKY[1]

UNITED NATIONS   NATIONS UNIES

LAKE SUCCESS, NEW YORK · FIELDSTONE 7-1100

10 March 1950
Professor Thomas C. Pollock,
Dean, College of Arts and Science,
New York University, New York, New York.

Dear Dean Pollock,

It was with a great deal of interest that I read your letter to the Editor of the New York Times, in which you indicate that Professor Cargill and you are editing the correspondence between Thomas Wolfe and the late Professor Watt when the former was teaching at New York University and the latter was Chairman of the Department of English.

As a graduate of Washington Square College, Class of 1933, I entered New York University in September 1929, and *subsequently was assigned to Mr. Wolfe's class in English I, Freshman Composition.* Naturally I, along with the other members of the particular section to which we were assigned, were not aware at the time that at some future date we would learn that it had been our good fortune to have met and studied with a person destined to become a potent force in American literature.

Some of my recollections are rather hazy at this time, particularly as to whether Mr. Wolfe was our instructor for both semesters of the 1929-1930 college year. Likewise, I had thought many times of how desirable it would be to reread Mr. Wolfe's criticisms and com-

[1] Bernard W. Kofsky, who is now connected with the Secretariat of the United Nations, was a student in Tom Wolfe's English I class, which met on Mondays, Wednesdays, and Fridays, from September 1929 to January 1930.

90

ments on our weekly compositions which we were required to produce and which, at the time, were such a chore. However, I have been unable to locate my compositions which have probably become lost in my moving about since I graduated (Hartford, Connecticut to Washington, D. C. and then to New York).

I am listing below some of my recollections of what were to me very pleasant hours with Mr. Wolfe:

1. Our class met on the top floor of the Commerce Building and with the crowd of students awaiting elevator service, considerable delay occurred in reaching class promptly. Mr. Wolfe was so impatient, that frequently he would use the steps rather than wait for an elevator. He would reach class perspired and dishevelled, and out of breath, and the first five minutes would be spent in waiting for him to regain his composure. He was always careless about his clothes and personal appearance; his hair always uncombed, long and curled in the back as though he hadn't seen a barber in months. I may add that he was so tall that he had to stoop in order to enter the class room. He generally carried an overloaded black brief case.

2. He was always late in returning our compositions, with the result that six weeks would often elapse before one would be returned with his corrections and/or comments, which were always made in red pencil. He explained that the delay resulted from his putting in so much time on his novel that he could find little time for reading our papers. He was working on *Look Homeward, Angel* at the time, and as the publication date approached, he would tell the class of his troubles in getting the final revisions completed and of his eagerness to see the book in print. When it finally appeared in the book shops, he offered to autograph copies for any members of the class purchasing the work. As I recall it very few members took advantage of his very gracious offer; I was one who failed to do so, to my continuing regret, but at the time I had to weigh the advantages of owning the book and buying future lunches or obtaining certain text books which I required. One gained the impression after listening to Mr. Wolfe, that the period of teaching was merely

a means to an end, namely, it served to provide him with the essentials of life until he could devote himself to writing exclusively.

3. Mr. Wolfe frequently called upon the class to present oral book reports, combining public speaking with the presentations. He would ask members of the class to go to the front of the room and present the reports, and sitting in the rear of the room, he would make his comments and lead a discussion of the book and comment upon the author and his style. I may add that while the class members were expected to read the collection of essays and literary works which served as the text book for the course, I recall that we had very few class discussions of such assignments.

The foregoing represent my immediate recollections of my associations with Thomas Wolfe and I hope that they will be of some assistance to Professor Cargill and you. Twenty years have elapsed since my freshman college days and memories are becoming hazy; if, however, I recall any other items of interest, I shall communicate with you again.

With every best wish for the successful publication of your book, I am,

Very truly yours,

Bernard W. Kofsky

THOMAS WOLFE, A REMINISCENCE

JAMES MANDEL[1]

I was introduced to Thomas Wolfe in 1929 by the Acting Dean of Washington Square College, Professor James Buell Munn. I was taking Munn's Bible course at the time and Tom was acting as the reader for the course. Wolfe was in straitened circumstances at that time. He was on leave of absence from his instructor's position at the Square and he was attempting to live on the few dollars he earned marking papers for Dean Munn and the five-hundred dollars advance against the royalties of his forthcoming "Look Homeward, Angel" which he had recently received from his publishers. When Tom Wolfe asked me to do some typing for him, I gladly acquiesced, realizing how valuable a close association with him would be. I don't know whether I had hoped to be a Boswell to this Johnson but I found myself doing just that. After an evening with him, I would rush home, and under the immediate influence of what he had said, I would enter his remarks and my observations in a notebook. One could not easily forget what Wolfe had told him, for his every word was filled with the intensity of the life he lived. He would pace the room, retrace his steps time and time again, muttering, gesticulating,— all goose flesh. He became completely oblivious of one's presence after a few minutes, so wrapped up was he in his own story.

He was like an adolescent when he spoke of the future. "I wonder how my book will be received, how much money it will bring me. . . . I wouldn't know how to spend more than six thousand a year. I'd like to have ten thousand books. I'd like to spend about a thousand dollars a year for books. . . . A two or three room apartment with a

[1] James, or "Jack" (as he was then called), Mandel was a student, as he tells us, in Dean Munn's Bible course when he became acquainted with Wolfe. The latter employed him as a typist while he was writing *Look Homeward, Angel*. Mr. Mandel is chairman of the Department of Biology and General Science in DeWitt Clinton High School, New York City.

Negro chef about forty years of age. . . . I love to eat you know. . . . I shall marry at seventy-three. Life is too short to be mixed up in nasty complications with other people (though he was involved in an affair with ["Mrs. Jack"] at the time). . . . A shack on a sea cliff in the summer," he went on, dreaming like a child. "Then Europe, perhaps once a year, a few months at a time, living liberally. Two thousand dollars is a sufficient sum for that. But it all depends upon the success of the book and if it should fail, it would hurt terribly."

Wolfe could not long bear the thought of the failure of the book, for he feared, more than anything else in the world, the criticism of his fellow instructors at the college. They could and did make life miserable for him because they were jealous of the fact that his book was going to be published. One of them had already told him that even were his book to sell a million copies it would mean nothing, for ". . . any book which wins popular acclaim is cheap." He venomously hated those who had succeeded in wounding him; once when he spoke of them, he snarled, "Is there anything he is not always belittling? He's the sharp satirist making fun of everything, everybody . . . envious, futile, that's what he is. He's strangling in the juices and poisons of his own body and he would carry others with him. He's a lonely and bitter man, and he would like nothing better than to gloat over me." Certainly, his relations with his colleagues were not very cordial; they felt his contempt, and they in turn teased and goaded him whenever the opportunity arose. "Ph.D's," he would counter, "seekers after small facts . . . would-be writers . . . a good student's work is better than the entire output of the English faculty! Why, one of those fellows has been writing a short story for the past ten years! Many of them talk of writing but they never write." His fellow instructors never forgave him, and even today they believe he is highly over-rated. "Only Clifton Fadiman thinks he is any good," said one of them whom I met a few years ago. Of course, the administration at the Square is still incensed at his biting descriptions in "Of Time and The River" of life at New York University, "The School of Utility Cultures."

Wolfe had decided opinions about writing. He felt that the night hours were the best for working because it was dark and quiet outside; that one should work steadily from five to fifteen hours daily. "There's no such thing as divine inspiration in writing," he said, "It's damn hard work, hours of sweat . . . my book took a year and a half of it." He believed that a writer had to have confidence in his own work, for "without it, it was impossible to continue; with it, a man should be able to write about twenty novels during his lifetime."

He always had a well-worn copy of Shakespeare's plays on his table and he was wont to read long passages from it as he walked the floor for long periods at a time. He would then return to his work with a vengeance to find a stream of words rushing to his lips with such speed that even with his mad and frenzied scribbling, he could not get it all down quickly enough on his ledger sheets. He had many such ledgers stacked away in boxes on the floor and in the closets. These books were filled with plays he had written at North Carolina University, at the Harvard Workshop, in New York. There were numerous poems he had dashed off, essays, short stories, — he had tried all the literary forms in his attempt to find the best way of expressing himself and finally he had decided upon the novel as the best medium. Those ledgers! Page upon page of illegible script! I would spend hours deciphering a few pages before I could begin to type the material and there were occasions when Wolfe himself could not read what he had written previously. One day, when I was working over one of these passages, I came across a fact that Wolfe had mentioned a few pages back. I called his attention to it and asked him whether he wanted me to type it or not. He looked at me a minute or two before he said anything and then, in a rather irritated tone, he remarked, "Of course include it!" Repetition was not harmful, he thought. If his emotions demanded this repetition at the time he was writing, then the material belonged in the book. As a matter of fact, he was sure that everything a man remembered should be included in his books. Though his editors urged him to discipline himself, to restrain the thousand and one tangential directions his story was taking, he was unable to do so. He would return from a visit to his publishers fuming and fretting because they had removed an entire chapter from his book. Like a chastened youngster, he would grumble for a few days before he conceded that they might be right. Wolfe simply could not bear to see those pages deleted. It was like amputating one of his limbs. His editors attempted to soothe his feelings by printing some of these chapters in magazine form. But to the day he died he was not convinced they were right.

Somerset Maugham was one of his favorite authors. He was quite lavish in his praise of "Of Human Bondage" because he believed "It came right from the guts, from the man's personal experience." He went on to add, however, that one of the few shortcomings in the book was its weak conclusion, its happy ending. "Philip Carey's marriage," he said, "is but a compromise with Mr. Maugham's true self, the morbid self which he is trying to hide by this subterfuge. A man would not really act that way." He thought that there were too many Philips in the world, too many people who interpret the complex things in life in complex ways and not in simple terms. "People," he said, "should try not to tangle themselves into a knot of morbid thoughts from which they cannot escape . . . the tendency will be to stir up a whirlpool of frustration. . . ." Was Wolfe really talking about himself, his own desperate struggle — he had many a gloomy moment! "It's too bad that Maugham gives himself so much to society, else he could have written more books like that. The ease with which he writes makes me certain of that."

And when I told Wolfe about the correspondence I had been carrying on with Maugham at that time, he thoughtfully commented, "There's something remarkable in the honest friendliness of this man to you. It is a wonderful thing. I had not had such an unusual thing happen to me when I was your age (twenty-one). Re-

[handwritten marginal notes by Thomas Wolfe on a student paper]

...ty, and beauty
"a bad desire"?
...you get my drift—
...one was interested
...the boy until the red
...ran out and fell on
...neck. But the
...greatest part of the
...life is in the...

(B)

I think your "writing" in this
paper is better than your
"thinking" & "feeling". Generally
your writing is plain and
clear, that is good. But
I believe you are wrong in
not seeing a greater similarity
between "the father of the
bible" and ~~...~~ "the father of
the four room apartment house"
— also, please try to picture
a "festering sore upon the
epidermis of the subsequent family
life". Can you do it?
& why weren't you the
one (out of 130) to wonder why
the Prodigal Son left home in
the first place & whether
the desire for pleasure...

AN EXAMPLE OF WOLFE'S THEME CORRECTION

Wolfe's comments on the outside sheet of a paper written by J. Lewis Mandel for Dean Munn's Bible class.

member, it is not knowing him that will make you a better writer, but your own hard work!"

The free, flowing, and easy style of Walt Whitman intrigued him. Whenever he wanted to praise your writing, he would say, "That has the Whitman sweep and breadth." Of Heywood Broun he remarked, "He showed great promise at one time but he is futile now." George Bernard Shaw he dismissed in a brief sentence, "People are tiring of him now. He's boring." What did he think of obscene books? "Pornographic books are inexcusable unless they illustrate life as a creative force. . . . Books that are written merely to illustrate the grime and grease of sex are disgusting." Do writers need to have profound minds? "No, the greatest writers have not been the greatest thinkers. They have different minds, that is all."

Breughel and Goya were his favorite painters and he spent much time in the art galleries of Europe studying their canvases. And why did he like Goya? ". . . because there is an evil lurking in all the sketches of the man." Indeed, a reason only a Wolfe would hold.

And why did he like to travel? "I travel to find myself. When I was twenty-one I yearned to travel. But at that age one isn't ready for it . . . one doesn't search for values then. . . . Today, when I get tired and irritable off I go to Europe. . . . But New York is my home. It's a center of culture and refinement. We have everything here for certain sums of money. Without money the city is cruel. When I come into money, I'll need no other place. . . . The people of France always think about money. In Italy, they are worse. The Germans are honest. . . . We spend money freely but the Europeans hoard it. But Vienna! The Viennese know how to live — easily. They love music and Schubert. (Wolfe liked to sing a tune from a Goethe poem, put to music by Schubert, which he had heard at the Schubert Festival in Vienna.) Yes, the Viennese really know how to live," he went on. "A man in Vienna inheriting an estate which provided an income of one-hundred and twenty-five dollars a month would stop working, spend his time at the movies, at the coffee houses, at the brothels . . . and the Viennese prostitute is the best of the lot. The French woman of the streets is hard and keen, always aware of the time. Her caresses are methodical as if to remind you that such love is being paid for by the tick of the clock. The American whore is usually tough. She, too, is always aware of the time. But the best of this type of womanhood lives in Vienna. There they are honest with their caresses and show some love for the man who is visiting them."

Trains had a fascination for him which he could never lose. The subway trains screeching around the turn at the 14th Street I.R.T. station struck a resonant chord in his body, for he seemed to vibrate sympathetically whenever he heard that harsh, shrill, sustained sound of steel wheels against steel rails. He described it as "A terrible cry of agony . . . ."

Teaching composition and an appreciation of literature to the pre-meds, pre-dents, and pre-laws at the Square was no easy task for any teacher; but for Wolfe the job was almost an impossible one. He was too conscientious about his work. He tried to make every one of his students respond to the beauty of a Shelley, but how could he when they were thinking of the rats they had just dissected, or the ether they were going to prepare in the organic chemistry lab the next hour? This period for them was the time to relax. Wolfe fought to gain their interest. He fumed and sputtered. He shouted at them to stop talking. He read poetry against a wall of constant murmur. He grew hoarse in a period and they wondered how long his voice would last under the strain. At the end of the lesson, he would leave the room perspiring, exhausted. Viewed from the present, it is remarkable that he did not become discouraged and resign his position at the college before he had achieved his success as a writer. But he stubbornly persisted in his efforts to train his students to appreciate a poem or an essay; and, by the end of the term, in fairness to him, it must be said that he had succeeded to a large extent where a more experienced teacher might have failed.

Wolfe never seemed to be able to get to class on time. His professor in the course in Advanced Writing given at North Carolina told a friend of mine that Wolfe had had the same failing in his days at the southern institution. The students would assemble, take their seats and the professor would begin his lecture on the topic of the day when a clattering noise would be heard on the stairway. It was Wolfe pounding away on the steel steps with his heavy mountaineer boots in his mad rush to get to class on time. The professor, not attempting to compete with the sound of violent movement outside, waited patiently until the long-legged giant entered the room and took his seat. He would then resume his lecture with the words "Now that the thunder has passed . . . ." The class would roar. But all this had no effect on Tom, for he would be late again the next day. So busy was he with his work as editor of the school literary publication that he seldom was aware of the fact that the period had already begun.

It may be the popular notion that Wolfe was so much interested in his writing that he neglected much of his work at the school. Nothing could be further from the truth. Though he dreaded the mountains of compositions he had to read each week, he could not rest before he had conscientiously corrected each theme. He felt that it was work worth doing. He sympathized with the creative agonies of his students; he was sorry for the difficulties many of them experienced in expressing themselves. He hurled himself into the job of correcting papers because he honestly realized that it was something which should and must be done. Certainly, he was not a shirker. Tom would go through each theme reading every word. He would underline every poorly chosen phrase, insert punctuation marks, remove others. He became so efficient in judging themes that he could determine the sex of the writer, for ". . . a girl's paper is easily recognized by its detailed punctuation and its careful wording . . . the man is careless, but it is from him that one expects flashes of strength and individuality."

On the back of every theme he marked, Tom wrote a long and

99

critical essay where the average instructor would have merely indicated the grade and a word of damnation or praise. Critics have thought Wolfe incapable of rendering judgment on a piece of writing, but these numerous and extensive criticisms which he wrote on every composition seem to prove otherwise. He could not leave a paper before he had dissected every creative impulse of the writer. I have at hand one of these criticisms which I think will bring out the point I am making. It follows: "I think your writing in this paper is better than your thinking and feeling. Generally, your writing is plain and clear. That is good. But I believe you are wrong in not seeing a greater similarity between the 'father of the Bible' and the 'father of the four-room apartment home.' Also please try to picture a *'festering sore on the equipoise of the subsequent family life.'* Can you do it? And why weren't *you* the one (out of 130) to wonder *why* the Prodigal Son left home in the first place, and whether the desire for pleasure, gayety, and beauty is a bad desire? Do you get my drift? — no one was interested in the boy until the old man ran out and fell on his neck. But the interesting part of the son's life is in the past."

Not only does the above criticism indicate Wolfe's ability to judge the student's writing and thinking, but it also gives us an added insight into his own character. Wasn't he too a prodigal son? He had left his home and his kin to make his own way in the world; and when he wanted to return, he found that he was not welcome. "You Can't Go Home Again!" And he was essentially a man who lived to satisfy his senses, who thought that the "desire for pleasure, gayety, and beauty" was all-important. He lived fully and at times exhausted himself in drinking bouts (during his days of affluence he purchased three quarts of Scotch a week according to one of the liquor men who supplied him), and [it was these] debauches, in hours of furious gratification of his senses, which probably, in the end, so lowered his resistance that he died of pneumonia and other complications at the age of thirty-eight. Like the prodigal, he felt that he was alone in the world, that no one was sincerely interested in him — although at that time he was in the midst of his violent love affair with the "Mrs. Jack" . . . of his novels.

The living quarters of a man frequently betray his character. In 1929, Wolfe lived in an old loft building near Fourteenth Street, just off Fifth Avenue. His apartment consisted of two rooms, one of them enormous in size as if to accommodate his elongated frame. Light flooded the entire place from a large window in the back. A work table stood in front of this window, and on it were drawings of costumes and sets which belonged to Aline Bernstein, the stage designer. (It is interesting to note at this point that Tom never spoke to me directly concerning . . . Aline Bernstein. It was obvious to me at the time for she seemed to come and go as she pleased. On several occasions, she worked on her designs at the long table near the window while Tom worked with me a short distance away in this work room. They seemed to take each other for granted in those days. Tom told me that Aline Bernstein was paying him for the use of the room. This was apparently an excuse to explain her presence in the apartment.)

A large, circular table with two old chairs occupied the center of the room. The table was cluttered with papers, ledgers, books, unwashed dishes, ashes, cigarette butts, pencils and glasses. The floor was littered. It was amazing how Wolfe could walk about without tripping over something. Dust covered the furniture. The large studio bed near the sink always needed to be made. Had Wolfe actually planned to make his place more disorderly, he could not have done a better job. He did not care one bit how his room appeared. And his personal appearance was no better when he was busy with his writing. Hair unkempt, dirt under his finger nails, grimy hands, soiled shirt, unpressed trousers! His face always had a pale and mealy look. He was not the Wolfe pictured on the jacket covers of his books. Not then. For while he worked he seemed to revert to the slovenly and careless habits of his Carolina days.

I remember one evening he offered to make a cup of tea for me. He boiled the water, awkwardly poured it into a cup, plunked in the tea ball, and set it down miraculously on the already crowded table. He then lit a cigarette and a moment later unconsciously flicked some ashes into the cup before I even had my first sip!

Wolfe was so deeply interested in himself that he rarely came out of his shell to consider the next fellow. He was careless because he was completely absorbed in his own thoughts. He was an egoist; there is no doubt of that. Ideas were boiling and distilling, sifting and vaporizing in his mind all the time. How could he know that he had flicked some ashes into a cup of tea! It was this intense interest in himself which probably accounts for the fact that he could remember incidents in his own life in the greatest detail.

After you had known Wolfe awhile, his personality affected you strangely. He had a dominating personality and his influence on the people he knew was tremendous. It was almost impossible to establish your own identity against the background of his character. Many of those he knew and described in his novels, he has left behind mumbling in pathetic tones. One of them, an outstanding figure in the world of the stage, belligerently refused to talk about him at all. Dissected by Wolfe in his books, still awed by his overshadowing personality, they whimper that they have lives of their own to live, things of their own to create, that they do not enjoy being considered part of the memorabilia of Wolfe.

Yet, despite his commanding personality, he was essentially a very timid fellow. One day, in 1927, after he had been away from the university for over a year on a trip to Europe, he stepped into the busy faculty office at the Square and asked the student clerk for his mail. The student requested his name. "Wolfe" was the answer. With a cursory glance at the hundreds of boxes, the young man returned, "No, no mail." Though Wolfe knew very well that he must have received many letters during his long absence, he walked away. Yes, timid, at a loss as to how to handle such a simple situation without hurting a stranger's feelings, he walked away!

Despite Wolfe's gargantuan size, he frequently reminded me of a gentle boy. When he came out of his shell, he was extremely decent. His honesty was beyond reproach. He often asked me whether he owed me any money for my typing. Such matters preyed upon his mind constantly.

He was extremely sensitive about his awkwardly long body. He was always afraid of being hurt, of being laughed at by the stranger on the street. And the remarks which young children made when they saw him for the first time always cut him deeply. One day, after I had told him of the torture I had suffered as a youth because of my lame leg, he revealed how touchy he was about his own incongruous figure. He could never understand why one man would laugh at another because of a physical handicap with which he had been cursed. "Is it really so, is it really true!" he shouted. "Yes, damn it, it's terribly true. It's because many people are so close to the baseline of the primitive themselves that they chuckle and laugh at us. It's the savage strain in them that makes them guffaw when they see us as ludicrous figures. And there's nothing we can do about it." Trying to make a joke of the whole matter, he sputtered, "Well, you're lame, I'm an elephant, and they're crazy!"

Such was the Tom Wolfe I knew.

MEMORABILIA

2 · HIS COLLEAGUES REMEMBER

"AND GLADLY TECHE ...."

ROBERT DOW [1]

30 December, 1949

Dear Oscar,

About Tom Wolfe. I am becoming increasingly embarrassed by my paucity of recollection, especially in connection with his coming to N.Y.U. I don't want to be embalmed in an erroneous footnote, but I am unable to do much about it. Perhaps I should seek comfort in becoming what I never expected to be, an exemplar of Wordsworth's "little, unremembered acts of kindness."

I knew Tom casually at Cambridge, chiefly through George Wallace, and I saw him a few times in New York, again casually and again through Wallace. From what Tom says in his letters to his mother (which I can't get hold of to check) and from what you say, it is clear that I at least suggested to him that he apply. When, where, how, and why I cannot say. Memory provides nothing beyond a kind of scrap of recollection that I talked with Wallace, especially as to whether Tom was properly equipped. I did not know that in addition to his writing courses he had taken others at Cam-

[1]After serving as an instructor in University College from 1922 to 1926, Robert Dow was appointed at the same rank at Washington Square College in 1928. He was Associate Professor of English and Assistant Director of Admissions at the time of his death, March 23, 1953.

bridge. I liked Tom although I didn't know him well and no doubt was concerned about his situation in life. At the time (I suppose it was the winter of 1923-24) I was a sweating young instructor at the Heights. The Square was rather vague to me although I did know Frank McCloskey a little. I don't see how I could have done more than make a suggestion to Tom. If there is anything specific in any of the letters, it might jog my memory. As I say, I liked Tom. To be honest, I must also say that I was a bit of a snob in those days. As a New Englander I couldn't understand what was supposed to be so damn wonderful about Harvard or why the outlanders reacted to it as they did. It was fashionable amongst strictly graduate students like myself to look with suspicion on the characters in the Baker Workshop. For all these reasons I don't doubt that although I liked Tom I thought he was a little odd and so didn't pay much attention.

I have only two distinct pictures of Tom at Harvard. I think that I first met him in some kind of eating joint where he, Wallace, and I happened to be at the same time. At any rate, we were subsequently strolling along Mass. Ave. just outside the yard in the moonlight, and Wallace, who was a little naive, kept saying over and over that Tom could recite the *Iliad* in Greek and asking him to do so. Tom naturally looked a little foolish but presently threw back his head and strode along singing it out in grand style. Later a play of Tom's ("Welcome to Our City" I think it was called) was done by the Baker workshop. I was one to surround him afterward for congratulations, and he was beaming and sweating and jumping up and down in obviously real pleasure. I probably saw him from time to time around Cambridge, but I don't remember.

All this was in the academic year 1922-23. I came to New York in September in the autumn of 1923 and so did Wallace. Through him I saw Tom several times sometime in the following winter. Again only two scenes realize themselves. One at the Albert Hotel, where Tom had a characteristically drab room, when we had had a few drinks and Tom and Wallace took to trying wrestling holds on each other. It should have been dangerous for Wallace, a small man, but wasn't. Tom was being very man about town with sexy remarks (as we said in the slang of those days) and innuendoes about the girl at the cigar counter in the hotel. I remember that I was somewhat surprised because Tom hadn't seemed like that at Cambridge and because it all seemed very like the travelling salesmen who are such hot numbers in a country hotel. Or used to be. The other scene is Tom and I walking from the Albert to 42nd St. in pursuit of a speakeasy which Tom had visited and thought superb but had only a vague notion about as to location. You can imagine that I was somewhat exhausted after practically running while Tom walked for some 34 blocks and poured out a ceaseless commentary. So, at 42nd, I decided that I'd had enough and went home to the Bronx. Of what he said I have no memory.

I think that I did not see Tom again until I came to the Square in 1928 after two years at Harvard. By then he was an entirely different person, slovenly, glowering, and looking like one pursued. We had no more than a hello acquaintance in the office. Apparently I made more impression on him than I thought, for in later years Terry would tell me that Tom had spoken of me or made some comment. I wonder if perhaps people did not have more effect on him than he did on them.

About Henry Carlton and George Nollen I know nothing. I know something about George Wallace. He had been a successful advertising man in Detroit, originally a graduate of Michigan. At the age of 40 or thereabouts he determined to sell his business, invest his money, and go to graduate school, chiefly with an eye to becoming a professional writer. He came to Harvard in the fall of 1922 and registered for Briggs' famous English 5 and several literature courses, in one of which I met him. He had an ungodly reverence for brains and talents of any kind, especially if connected with literature, and could hardly believe he was at last in such a community. Naturally he was rusty on study and lacking in background so that he sweat blood over his work with only average results. As I

106

remarked, he was a little naive, although it may have been simply the naivite of inexperience. He thought all the people in the Baker workshop were demi-gods, especially Wolfe. At that, he may have been more perceptive than some of the rest of us. In the fall of 1923 he came to New York to take writing and other courses at Columbia. At the end of that year he went off to Europe for some time and returned to settle in Concord, Mass. I lost touch at that point. Someone, I think Terry, told me that he died in the course of the thirties. Possibly Terry has been in communication with the widow and the two sons. Wallace was a generous, kindly, enthusiastic man, somewhat pathetic in his purpose to convert his life, and I can believe he was a most warming friend to Wolfe.

I see that I have told you more about myself than about Wolfe. Perhaps that is the way of reminiscence. As you see, I knew him mostly through Wallace. His departure in 1924 and my work at the Heights and later at Harvard meant that I did not see Tom, except after I came to the Square.

Recently, Winthrop Ranney, professor of English at the Heights, told me an anecdote about Wolfe at Harvard. Ranney was then much interested in writing and knew the writing crowd at Cambridge more than I did. He might have some interesting material. Richmond Bond, professor of English at North Carolina, who taught in our summer school last summer, acted in Tom's play at Cambridge. He might have something to add.

Apologies for scantiness. Happy New Year!

Bob Dow

TOM WOLFE: PENANCE NO MORE

HENRY T. VOLKENING[1]

I have a thing to tell you:
  Something has spoken to me in the night, burning the tapers of the waning year; something has spoken in the night; and told me I shall die, I know not where. Losing the earth we know for greater knowing, losing the life we have for greater life, and leaving friends we love for greater loving, men find a land more kind than home, more large than earth.
  Whereon the pillars of this earth are founded, toward which the spirits of the nations draw, toward which the conscience of the world is tending — a wind is rising, and the rivers flow.

                                                            THOMAS WOLFE

It was at the end of a dreary winter's day some twelve years ago. I had not long been teaching at New York University on Washington Square, though long enough already to have lost some early unreasonable enthusiasm.

One of the instructors, a poet of sorts, seriously asked, "How do *you* teach appreciation?" And a huge, black-haired man at a desk nearby squirmed and looked incredulous. He had just returned from Europe, they told me, to teach in the spring term, though he'd been here before.

Then the minister's son from the open spaces, one of the most self-assured and emancipated of our staff, started to bellow at us for the hundredth time that Samuel Butler's "The Way of All Flesh" was the best novel in English, nearest to the essential bitter truth and so forth. I rose for rescue toward the water-cooler, just as the huge man with the wild black hair tilted his head to bellow back, "And since then, by God, nothing whatsoever has been written!" He jumped up, and with what seemed like but three giant strides, stood over me at the water-cooler, looking fierce, his whole

---

[1] Formerly Instructor in English, Washington Square College, Henry T. Volkening is now an authors' agent in New York City.

face compressed, swaying with hands on his hips. "Look," he said, pointing his finger into my eye, "I don't know you but you're new here, aren't you? I'm Thomas Wolfe and it's time to eat something, isn't it? Let's get out of here. I know a good place." And his face relaxed as we turned to go. "Tired?" he asked, smiling suddenly.

By three of the next morning he had stopped talking, and after that we often escaped together, having found the way. Sometimes others joined us, and always Tom talked, endlessly, joyously, bitterly, humorously, lyrically, with never any compromise with what he saw as the truth, never at a loss for words or subject, and never, of course, with the slightest regard for the lesser vitality and strength of his auditors, whom he would always leave in a state of happy and dazed collapse.

But there were times when he became quiet and confidential. Then he would tell of his hopes and longings, of little amenities and pleasures, of his tastes and friends and affections. Then he would no longer be tortured by the demon of the writer in him, and he would be kind, compassionate, and just. It was this side of him that is unknown, that appears rarely in his books, and that was as much a part of him as the ruthless and driven artist in him, who never knew peace or rest.

Those were the days when he was quite poor, or at least felt himself to be, when I used often to go to see him, sometimes alone, and sometimes with Natalie, my wife, at his "hole," as he called it, on West Eleventh Street, where he had a perfectly tremendous and very attractive three-room apartment, a part of which Aline Bernstein occasionally used as a workshop for her stage-designing. The place was in incredible disorder, as Tom's homes usually were, with a minimum of furniture, and with manuscripts and books and hundreds of "Freshman themes" thrown everywhere.

There he would entertain his visitors, often in a bathrobe, or in blue shirtsleeves, with talk, apologies, and tea — always tea, on a big cluttered table, served in enough unmatched cups to go almost around, with lump sugar from the original package, or from the table. And he'd pace about, distressed at having been interrupted in his work, and yet very happy.

At first he was principally concerned with his teaching and with what he conceived to be the false values of many of his colleagues. Their preciosity, their limited experience, their knowing small-talk, spoken in a kind of code, and their concern with tea-cup tempests — these things, and most particularly their prejudices and bad literary judgments, he found hateful in them. "Look," he would say, pointing to a shelf of books above his working table, "there in one small row is much of the best that has ever been written, and half of those they've never really read." And there was Burton's "Anatomy of Melancholy," Melville's "Moby Dick," Dostoevsky's "Brothers Karamazov," Heine, Shakespeare, Donne, Goethe, Homer, Plato, Euripides, Walt Whitman, Joyce's "Ulysses" (freely marked-up), the Bible, Swift, Boswell's "Johnson," Voltaire's "Candide," Milton, Coleridge (including the essays), Herrick, De Quincey, Anderson's "Winesburg, Ohio," Defoe's "Moll Flanders," Bennett's "Old Wives' Tale," Fielding's "Tom Jones," and a few others which I have forgotten.

The actual classroom work he enjoyed hugely, but he was none the less always talking of the day when he would be freed from the economic necessity of teaching. Most of his students discouraged him profoundly, though I never heard him say an unkind word about any one of them. I believe that they thoroughly disgusted him, but he was always patient with them, gave them of his very "heart and guts," and was conscientious in his study of their efforts at composition, to a degree which was surely appreciated by very few. Chiefly he was sorry for them, especially for the "tortured in-tellectuals," which, he said, "so many Jewish students are."

Tom was then in such difficult financial circumstances that he could not afford to do more than dream of complete freedom from his duties at the college. (He always thought of himself as being poor, for that matter, and as coming of poor parents, though his father is said to have left a very substantial fortune, which was subsequently all lost.) He had only just graduated from a room on Eighth Street, which he described as being a mere attic in a deserted house, from the ground floor of which he had nightly to chase the derelicts, of whom there were often a dozen, for fear of their leaving cigarettes that would burn him to death. Then he would barricade the house, and get to work again on themes, and on "Look Homeward, Angel," a large part of which he wrote on those nights, with a can of beans, coffee, cigarettes, and long shadows for company.

He worked like a man literally possessed, impatient with every petty interruption, so forgetful of time and friends that he would rarely remember an engagement for more than an hour or two, and would resent anyone's efforts to "tie him down" to a social obligation, much though he wanted companionship. I remember his phoning me at eleven o'clock one evening, to ask me if I could have some dinner with him, embarrassed and confused to discover the hour.

Work, and more work, that was his only god, and his only faith was in his work, and in himself. That was why he was so bitter against not only every critic who doubted his power, but even against people who ignored his efforts, or who held views which, if sound, would by necessary inference impugn his own convictions. His attacks were often based upon a chance remark of the victim, or upon an attitude or a look, so that his conversation and writing were packed with a most unjust destruction of character, when it was only some characteristic or mannerism that had unpredictably annoyed him. Whenever he detected affectation, dullness, sterility, duplicity, or formalism, his annihilating rhetoric slaughtered wholesale, in the names of integrity and justice.

The aesthetes who needed what they called inspiration before they could work, and who would of course never work, he despised as much as he did those who would have literature serve an irrelevant cause, such as Communism or Fascism. The "business boost-ers," invariably caught in their self-made periodic crashes; lawyers, with their frustrating technicalities and machinations and delays; the gossip columnists and their readers; "the cafe-society swine, with a sense of values so distorted that, like the giraffe, you couldn't be-lieve it if you hadn't seen it"; dentists and doctors; actors, for their sole interest in boring you with being either somebody else or nobody at all; "the whole damned theater crowd"; most modern painters, "painting theories because they are too incompetent to paint man or nature"; self-styled music lovers; pedagogues, opera singers, and "men who wear pearl-gray hats"; psychoanalysts and their pathetic patients, "suffering from nothing but too much money and too little to do, without the sense to know that it is all in Plato, in understandable language not especially manufactured for the trade"; those mystics "to whom their own otherwiseness is sufficient evidence of the existence of a God, maybe even with a beard"; women, for "their inherent incapability of detached and imper-sonal thought," and for "their feeling a right to possess you forever when you've done them a favor, especially a sexual favor"; tele-phone chatterers, other than himself; the women's-club favorites; most Southerners, as distinguished from the South; all the sophisti-cates among the writers, except Aldous Huxley; book reviewers, on principle; creative critics, who, "having no talent themselves, anni-hilate beautifully those who do"; and those people of Asheville who were bitterly disappointed that they could not threaten to horse-whip him for their not being in "Of Time and the River"; — all these he castigated with a wonderful nobility of passionate invective.

Still, despite his talent in the character of a vengeful god, Tom's lighter satire always seemed to me more truly like him. There was the picture postcard from Atlantic City, for instance, exhibiting the broad rear-ends of four monstrous bathing beauties, on which he had written, "Here for the weak-end." He used to compare Atlan-tic City with Washington, D.C., to the disadvantage of the latter, as "last resorts for the amusement of ciphers." One Fourth of July he wrote, from New York, "The free Americans have been shooting off firecrackers all day; it's about all they can do." From England: "I am looking forward to a real old fashioned London Christmas — that is to say fog, rain, and a sodden wet woolly stuff they call air." Little academic notes: "Did you know they are dividing N.Y.U. up into colleges according to the Oxford plan? I've been appointed Master of Hoggenheimer Hall.— The year at N.Y.U. is over and gone (with my prayers) to oblivion. When I saw the boys last many had turned slightly green, yellow, and purple from stored-up poison and malice." A suggestion to the traveler: "Why don't you go to Italy and follow the spring north? It would be so pleasant getting cheated in Sorrento in April." And another: "I am glad to be out of France — the people are cats: I don't mean anything against them, they are cats. . . ."

At times like these, I think, he was his lovable self. But when a black mood was on him, induced always by some trouble or irritation that kept him from his work, and on occasion exaggerated by too much alcohol, he would descend upon even his best friends with an unforgivable ferocity absolutely unwarranted by anything they had said or done. And these tirades would be the more embarrassing because they were invariably followed by stuttering and painful contrition, and by great lengths of effort to make amends.

He did have a genuine interest in his friends, and in all they thought or did. I remember with what fascination he entered into my plans for an extended European trip which my wife and I were outlining late in 1928, how he would pore over maps with us late into the night with as much enthusiasm as if this were going to be his own trip, telling of places and pictures and sights that we especially should not miss: Naples, Pompeii, Sorrento, Rome, Florence, Vienna, Munich, Nuremberg, Montreux, Bath, York, the English Lakes, the Trossachs, Fountains Abbey; the paintings of Michelangelo, Rembrandt, Durer, Gruenwald, Hals, and particularly Breughel. In February, 1929, he even wrote a spontaneous little note from the Harvard Club, on what must have been one of his few leisure evenings: "I'm working on a huge book for Henry and Nat — a Glutton's Guide, a Sensualist's Handbook of seven countries with all about where to eat, drink, sleep — and how to avoid Rhodes Scholars, bedbugs, Ph.D.'s — and other itinerant vermin. You can call the book Profiting, by Tom's Mistakes."

A month later Tom came to see us sail at midnight on the *Vulcania*. It was a happy time for him, for Scribner's had accepted "Look Homeward, Angel," after several other publishers had turned it down. His good will, toward us and toward the world, was boundless, and he had a great affection for the ship too, for when he had last been abroad he had come home on her, on her maiden voyage. We toasted one another and explored the boat from bow to stern. Tom showed me what had been his quarters, "with three miserable wops, only slightly deloused, and always seasick." And he introduced me to his steward, to the bartender, and to a host of sailors, who seemed to remember him, and acknowledged his effusive greetings with the puzzled and frightened look of people about to be engulfed. We visited our little inside cabin, which, I thought, disappointed Tom in being not quite regal. He had somehow vaguely believed that we would be traveling in one of those private-veranda apartments reserved for "the fabulous women of the fabulously rich." It was on these apartments and their women that he glued devouring eyes. (I always thought he looked at women as if they were juicy steaks.) As we slowly drew from the pier, we could see his huge and lonely figure towering above the others, his arm waving awkwardly until the night swallowed him.

We heard from Tom, not frequently but usually at length, for writing letters bothered him so much that when he once managed to get around to the task he filled page after page in a kind of frenzy to make quick and worthy amends for weeks of silence. From New York, July 4:

> Your letters and postals have given me the greatest pleasure. I cried out for joy at your rapturous letter from Vienna: I had a great personal pride in it, as if I had discovered the place. . . Long, long ago

I wrote you . . . wrote page after page, but never finished it . . .
My other letter was filled with news — which I've forgotten. I feel
splendid, and am fresh and fat. My proofs are coming in, my story
appears in the magazine next month (get it in England if you can —
Scribner's for August), book's out in the fall, and Scribner thinks it a
grand thing and that it will go. I hope it makes a splash — not a flop!
— but that it splashes me with a few dollars. Also, writing some short
stories that they have asked me to write. . . . Loaded to the decks with
my new book. — Thank God I'm thirty pounds overweight, it's going
to kill me writing it.

Again from New York, August 9:

Please forgive me for not having written you more and oftener. I've
been in Maine and Canada for several weeks. . . . Maine was lovely
and cool. — I was at a wild little place on the coast. I fished, corrected
proofs, and read John Donne and Proust all day long. . . . I am going
to buy an island there surrounded by woods and the Atlantic Ocean.
— I have already saved $1.25, and need only $2,998.75 more.

I envy you everything on your trip except the hordes of tourists who
are, you say, beginning to swarm around you. I note you are going to
Paris. . . . Whenever I think of the French . . . I control myself and
mutter "Voltaire! Voltaire!"— And, after all, that is how a civilization
should be judged — by its best, not by its worst, but its worst is pretty
damned terrible, and unfortunately it requires superhuman fortitude
and vision to see through to Ronsard when one is struggling to escape
the snares of ten thousand petty rascals. Nevertheless, I have thought
of France recently more than of any other country. — It is physically
the most comfortable and civilized of nations, and its highest and best
spiritually is magnificent. The greatest evil in the national temper, I
think, is "glory"— what they call "la gloire."— It accounts for the flag
waving, "France has been betrayed," speech making, singing the
Marseillaise, going to war, et cetera. — It represents what is cheap and
melodramatic in them. I could go on like this indefinitely, but you
can hear the other side from any of the fourteen thousand American
epic poets, novelists, dramatists, composers, and painters now in Paris.
They all "understand" France, and will point out my treason. . . .

My story came out in the August Scribner's — also a picture of the
author in the back and a brief write-up of his romantic life — how he
has a "trunkful of MSS.," "forgets all about time when working,"

and "goes out at three A.M. for his first meal of the day." I was more madly in love with myself than ever when I read it.

I had expected convulsions of the earth, falling meteors, suspension of traffic, and a general strike when the story appeared — but nothing happened . . . . Nevertheless I am still excited about it. Proofs of the book will be finished in a day or two. The Book-of-the-Month Club heard of the book. . . . There's not much hope of its being their selection. They have pure and high-minded judges like William Allen White and Christopher Morley — and they may find some of the stuff too strong. Besides I am an unknown writer and they have hundreds of MSS. — but if! but if! but if! *Then,* of course, I should immediately accept the Abe Shalemovitch Chair in Anglo-Saxon Philology at N.Y.U. . . .

Scribner's have been magnificent, their best people have worked like dogs on the thing — they believe in me and the book. To have found a firm and association with men like this is a miracle of good luck. . . . I tremble, now that the thing's done. — I loathe the idea of giving pain, it never occurred to me as I wrote, it is a complete piece of fiction but made, as all fiction must be, from the stuff of human experience. Perhaps I may have to wear false whiskers and smoked glasses. Again perhaps no one will notice it. This too is a complicated thing about which I shall talk to you.

I am aching with a new one — it's got to come out of me, I loathe the idea of not writing it, and I loathe the idea of writing it — I am lazy, and doing a book is agony — sixty cigarettes a day, twenty cups of coffee, miles of walking and flying about, nightmares, nerves, madness — there are better ways, but this, God help me, is mine.

Forgive me — I have talked only about myself. . . .

In September we returned home and we soon saw him again. He talked about our trip, about himself, and about the book which was to be off the press in a few days. There were many dinners and visits, and he seemed, on the whole, quite happy.

I remember his infectious and childlike excitement on the day when Scribner's window first displayed "Look Homeward, Angel," when he told of pacing back and forth in front of the piles of gay covers, admiring the colors, the arrangement, and the prominence accorded "this baby of mine." He frightened other passersby, and attracted the attention of the cop on the beat by his "strange weavings and ogling." He stopped in at book stores to ask whether people were buying it, and avidly read all the reviews he could lay his hands upon, cursing every one that did not shower it with unqualified praise. He told of riding on a bus next to a girl who held a copy of the book, which was the first time he believed that people were really reading it, and of his not quite daring to speak to her, though he never so much in his life wanted to speak to anyone. And finally he began to see, despite initial misgivings, despite neglect in some quarters, and despite some stupid vilifications, that his first child had not been stillborn, and that his faith in himself and his work had substance in the eyes of the world.

I saw Tom often that fall, usually in his tremendous one-room "hole" on Fifteenth Street, just west of Fifth Avenue, with its long row of casement windows facing north on comparatively quiet backyards. His book was "selling"; it brought him some money and a bank account, and the chance to lay his too long deferred plans to relieve himself of the burdens of teaching. Those critics and writers whose opinions he valued were showering encomiums upon him with a liberality that should have gladdened the heart and soul of any man. But, paradoxically enough, it seemed to be this very success which distressed him most, which drove him to work even harder upon his next book, while misgivings about its reception were already crowding themselves into his spirit. The suggestions by some of the reviewers that in "Look Homeward, Angel," so patently autobiographical, he had possibly written himself out, maddened him with a determination to prove to others the faith he had in himself that as long as he might live he could never write himself out. He would "show them too that he could compress, maybe like Dostoevsky," that he could write short stories to conform to "any damned acceptable pattern they wanted." He said he would write a Gargantuan fable for them, without a recognizable person in it, with New York as setting, portraying the struggles of an artist against the attempts of literary people to cheapen and kill him: a modern "Gul-

117

liver's Travels" that would make Swift seem all sweetness and light. And he would even scores too with those noble Southerners of the old school who were driving him insane with their scores of threatening letters, and this he would do by becoming so famous that these same people would be "building monuments to me, comparing me to O. Henry (hah!), naming their children after me, and nigger children too (hah!), and stuffing me with food, just so they can get a good look at me, and tell me of my contribution to the great literature of the South (hah!). But I do wish," he would say with a sudden sadness, "that they would try to understand, and that they would let me alone."

One day he phoned me to come over to help him resist "a boy from back home" who was about to stop in to sell him some life insurance. There was a comical desperation in his plea, for the simple fact was that he could not have paid premiums, and yet he could not deny people on merely logical grounds. And another time he spoke of "the strange songs and melodies in my head, which I intend some day to set down"; strange they must have been, for he seldom spoke of or listened to music, or even hummed or whistled. He often talked about women, of those who came to see him and to stay with him, of the many he had slept with and the none he had known, of the two worlds in which men and women live, speaking different languages, never to understand each other.

But he was far from being a Don Juan. I have always felt that his wild habits were nothing more than one expression of an insatiable and overwhelming vitality. At heart he was pathetically and naively domestic. He wanted, or thought he wanted, a wife, a home, and children. "It is only through his work and children that man can achieve immortality, and even the work, no matter how good, will die, in time. You see what I mean, don't you?" He wrote me once, "I have begun fondly to meditate a loving wife, my own — this time! — and a few little ones, but where to start searching for these simple joys is beyond me." He profoundly envied the supposedly quiet and simple lives of the happily married. "I notice," he said in a letter, "that people who have never been alone for five minutes in their lives cheerfully banish you to solitude, assure you there's no life like it, how they envy you, and it is all for the best, after all, et cetera. But I've had thirty years of it!"

The tension and speed of his life continued unabated. He went everywhere where life was: along Fourteenth Street, "one of the most horrible and helpless streets in the world, where the faces have lost every last trace of human dignity and striving"; and into the wild wastes of "endless Brooklyn, a city so desolate as to be unbelievable"; into, through, and out of every subway in New York; to neighboring towns and cities; into Pennsylvania, where some of his ancestors had lived, unaccountably fearful of finding a Jewish name among them, and relieved at finding none; to baseball games when Babe Ruth was playing, to enjoy his "tremendous rhythmic swats"; to park benches to "stare at my navel, and feel vaguely uneasy, like all Americans, that I was not doing something"; to "lit'ry teas" when he could not help himself, to confound anemic dilettantes, and probably also to scare them nearly to death, by shouting parts of the "Iliad" at them, in Greek, to prove that he knew what he was talking about and that they didn't; through the chasms of Wall Street during the stock market crash of 1929, expecting the bodies of suicides to fall upon him; to restaurants and speakeasies without number; and then back to his "hole" again, to reflect upon and to tell and to write about it all, and to lament the sad fact that "the artist can never freely enjoy any experience, for he is forever studying life in terms of translating it into something finer. And yet," he would say, "the artist must have first-hand experience. That is one thing I never could quite understand about Irving Babbitt, though he was in many ways a great man. I would rather listen to Coleridge, who comes to me sometimes in dreams, shadowy in a darkened room, sitting at a piano, looking at me — and like me."

The spring of 1930 brought the end of Tom's last year of teaching, and he escaped to Europe from troubles at home, for what he hoped, as he always hoped, would be a rest and a vacation, but which turned out to be a time of hectic adventures and heartache more terrible than any he had known before.

I first heard from him in July, from Montreux:

> There is nothing to do here. I read a great deal, an English fellow named Shakespeare, the poems of Heine and Gooty, Donne , , , also Racine and Pascal — both sublime and dull.
>
> My book is minutely outlined, and I have learned so much about brevity and condensation that it will not be over 600,000 words long. I am quite serious. It will be a very good book if I live to finish it. There are four parts and each is longer than an average novel.
>
> I am reading "War and Peace" at the repeated suggestion of Maxwell Perkins. He is quite right about it: it is a magnificent book. . . .

In September came a letter from Strasbourg:

> I've written you three enormous letters, none of which I have been able to finish. In the first two I couldn't say anything I wanted to say, and in the last one I said everything. . . . I have had some of the worst and also, I think, some of the best moments of my life these last four or five months. On the whole it's been a pretty bad time for me, but I am now out of the woods. For eight weeks now I have not spoken with one person that I knew — yes, I did see for one night a man I knew. . . . It would be better if I had never seen him at all: he has played me one series of shabby tricks this summer, and also made some very pretty speeches about character, courage, honor, et cetera. . . . He . . . saw romance where it did not exist — or if it did exist, it existed in bloody and sorrowful depths that he will never fathom.
>
> Now I am going to a place where I shall have a place of my own and there are two or three real friends (I believe) that I can trust and talk with. I need both. I have been alone long enough now, it has been bitter medicine, but it has done me good, and I am back on my feet again. . . .

In January, 1931, arrived a young book from London:

> I am rapidly becoming a great authority on the subject of *Work,* because I . . . have done some —"and penance more will do." By the way, that would be a good title for almost any book —"Penance More"— for that, I think, is what it takes to write one. . . . I have not only worked but I have worked with spiritual bellyache, toothache,

headache — as well as with something like a virulent abscess just over my left lung, and I think now that I shall probably work under almost any kind of conditions. . . . Buy a book written by one Anthony Trollope, Esq., who wrote about ninety-seven other books in addition. It is called "An Autobiography." . . . . Brother Trollope with great good humor and some cynicism describes his methods of work, and tells how he managed to write fifty or sixty novels while riding all over Ireland and England in the Civil Service, going hunting twice a week, entertaining many friends, and in general leading a hell of an active life. . . .

I shall never write fifty books or learn to write in railways or on boats, nor do I think it is desirable, but it is certainly a damned good idea to get ideas of steady work, and I think this is a good book to read. I am able to do thirty or thirty-five hours a week — thirty-five hours is about the limit and if I do that I am pretty tired. If a man will work — really work — for four or five hours every day, he is doing his full stint. Moreover, I find very little time for anything else. — I practically spend twenty-four hours getting five hours work done: I go out very little. But it soon gets to be a habit. — I wish sometimes I was less homesick, less lonely, and sometimes less heartsick; I could certainly imagine better conditions for work, and I am firmly decided (between us!) that the "going-abroad-to-write business" is the bunk. — I went to Paris Christmas; it is one of the saddest messes in the world to see all these pathetic _____ who are beginning to get ready to commence to start. Why a man should leave his own country to write — why he should write better in Spain, France, England, or Czechoslovakia than at home is quite beyond me. . . . It seems to me that one of the most important things a writer can have is tenacity — without that I don't see how he'll get anything done. Someone told me a year or two ago that the pity about modern writers is that the people who have the greatest talent for writing never write, and an embittered and jealous Irishman told me that one of the people Joyce wrote about in Ulysses was a much better writer than Joyce if he wanted to write — only he didn't want to. All this, in the phrase of my innocent childhood, "makes. . . ."

There can be no talent for any writing whatever unless a man has power to write: tenacity is one of the chief elements of talent — without it there is damned little talent, no matter what they say. Which I suppose is only another way of saying Arnold's dogma: Genius is energy. I think I would agree that the best writers are not always the people with the greatest natural ability to write. For example, I have never felt that Joyce was a man with a great natural ability. — I don't believe he begins to have the natural ease, fluency, and interest of, say, H. G. Wells. But he had an integrity of spirit, a will, and a power to work that far surpasses Wells. — I don't mean mere manual and quantity work; Wells had plenty of that, he has written one hundred books. — But I mean the thing that makes a man do more than his best, to exhaust his ultimate resources. That is the power to work and that cannot be learned — it is a talent and belongs to the spirit. At any rate, the only way out . . . is work — work under all circumstances and conditions. I am sure of that!

But . . . I am not nearly so easy and certain as I sound — but I am sure what I said about working is right. I do not know whether what I am doing now is good or bad — the impulse and the idea are very good — but, as *always* between us, I think I have been on the verge of the deep dark pit for two years, and I am just beginning to get away from it. I am tired of madness and agony. I am willing to let the young generation have a fling of it — after all, I'm an old fellow of thirty and I deserve some peace and quiet. If work will do it I'll come through: I'll work until my brain and the last remnant of energy go. I suppose some people would say I have never spared others, but I should say that I never spared myself, and on the whole I think other people have done pretty well by me. I have given away what I would never sell if I had it again for diamond mines — years out of the best and most vital period of my life — and I find myself today where I was ten years ago, a wanderer on the face of the earth, an exile, and a stranger, and by God, I wonder why! I can't help it if it sounds melo-dramatic — it is the simple truth. . . . I am tired of . . . Europe. . . . I know it is all wrong — but where to live on that little strip of 4000 miles is the question. . . . I confess now to a low craving for compan-ionship, the love and affection of a few simple _____ and eve-nings spent by the ingle nook. . . .

Most of the people I like and a great many I dislike are in New York, but I can't go back there: it would be like walking around with perpetual neuralgia at present — the place is one vast ache to me — and I've offered quite enough free entertainment to the millions of people who having no capacity for feeling themselves spend their lives on the rich banquet some poor hick from the sticks (like myself) has to offer: I've learned a few things and the next time the _____ want to see a good show they're going to pay up!

I am going to see the Four Marx Brothers tomorrow with my English publisher — they are here in the flesh and the swells have suddenly discovered they were funny — so I suppose I shall have to listen to the usual horrible gaff from the Moderns: "You know there's something very grand about them — there really is, you know. I mean there's something sort of epic about it, if you know what I mean. I mean that man who never says anything is really like Michelangelo's Adam in the Sistine Chapel, he's a Very Grand Person, he really is, you know, they are really *Very* Great Clowns, they really are, you know," et cetera, et cetera, et cetera. . . . The dear Moderns, you will find, are cut from the same cloth and pattern all over the world. — Unplatitudinously they utter platitudes, with complete unoriginality they are original. Whenever they say something new you wonder where you heard it before, you believe you have not heard it before, you are sure you have heard it forever, you are tired of it before it is uttered, the stink of a horrible weariness is on it, it is like the smell of the subway after rush hours. . . . I am tired of these weary _____: they hate life, but they won't die.

The literary business in America has become so horrible that it is sometimes possible to write only between fits of vomiting. If you think that is extreme I mention a few names. . . . Keep away from them: don't talk about . . . writing to anyone, don't tell anyone what you're writing, and go with doctors, architects, bootleggers — but not with writers. This is not bitter advice: it is simply good advice — no one has ever written any books about America — I mean the real America — I think they bring out ten or twenty thousand books a year, but no one has ever written about America, and I do not think the "writers" will. . . .

I did not hear again from Tom, until one morning in spring he phoned from the end of Brooklyn to tell me that he had just docked. We met in Tom's room at the Prince George Hotel, and set out to spend the day, drinking and eating. It was impossible to leave him for mere office appointments, when it was so obviously refreshing to his soul to tell of his happiness to be home, with all of the bitter experiences of Europe behind him, feeling freed again, for a little while at least, from intanglements and madness and despair. His

123

chief anxiety was to get out of Manhattan as soon as possible, where old wounds might reopen, and to find an apartment on Brooklyn Heights, where "people would let me alone, for the mere name of Brooklyn frightens them with visions of great distances."

He soon found spacious quarters, in no less than two floors of a house with a pleasant backyard, not on the Heights, but no farther than a long walk from there. Later he moved to Columbia Heights, to a place only a few minutes from Brooklyn Bridge, across which he often walked at sundown. And from the Heights he finally came back to the city and rented an apartment on one of the upper floors of a modern First Avenue building. In 1935 he took a short trip to Europe, principally to spend some small German royalties which could not be exchanged, and to enjoy his fame in Germany, where, he wrote, "People overwhelmed and exhausted me with friendship, et cetera. The only place I was ever famous. . . ." There he enjoyed "all the social gaiety I have missed for the last thirty-four years." The newspapers even took pictures of him getting on and off trolleys, he as big as the trolleys, and everyone roaring with delight.

When "Of Time and the River" finally appeared, it was an instant success, so that Tom was for a time financially happier, and better able to live and dine well, even extravagantly. But troubles seemed to pursue Tom Wolfe more than they did most men. There was a suit against him brought by a former agent, about which I thought he was both needlessly generous and relentlessly bitter, and a libel action which brought him more into conflict with his flabbergasted attorneys than with the plaintiff, and a suit which he had to institute for the recovery of some manuscripts which he had very unwisely given into the possession of a young boy. His disrespect for the law became almost epic, for these troubles kept him from having a free mind for his work, they cost him more money than he could afford, and they brought about several lamentable clashes which had only remotely to do with their causes. There were few occasions when I met or talked to him when he was not in a murderous rage about some recent interview with a lawyer.

But of those few occasions, one especially stands out in my mind. It was in the early summer of 1937, late in the afternoon, immediately following a brief but terrific rain and thunderstorm. As I walked down First Avenue I saw him standing at the window of his apartment, high over the city, leaning upon the open upper sash, smoking vigorously, as his searching eyes took in the beauty of the sudden clearing at sunset. He spoke, when I arrived, of the "clean glory" of the scene, and I felt that it must have refreshed his very soul, for that evening he too saw and felt "cleanly," and forgot his struggles for a few hours. At dinner he talked of his plan to go south to live for a while on a farm outside of Asheville, with a good Negro servant all to himself, and with a sign at the front entrance: "Visitors welcome, without firearms." He was apprehensive about his reception, but he hoped that time would have softened much bitterness, and that there would be few "envious and defeated people." He spoke of his disgust at some hardhearted intellectuals for their sentimental sympathy for far-off Loyalist Spaniards about whom they knew nothing. "The miseries of home, I suppose, are not romantic enough, not noble enough, and, above all, oh dear yes, not ideological enough." He talked of death, and asked if I had ever seen a man die; when I told him yes, he asked me to tell him everything I saw. "Did he give any sign of — of — anything? I suppose not. I suppose no one ever really has."

Late that night we walked to Scribner's, where he gathered some mail and brought down a copy of "The Story of a Novel," which he autographed under a street lamp on Fifth Avenue. I never saw him again.

He phoned me once after that, to say that he had just changed publishers. He seemed pained and confused and elated about it, and he sought to justify his action by telling of advice he'd had from some writers organization, of the folly of mixing business and friendship, and of his hope that he had lost no friends who mattered. He felt unwell, he said, and very tired.

Some months later he went west to Washington, where he'd always wanted to go, and there he contracted the pneumonia which ultimately led to his death after a brain operation in Baltimore, in the same hospital in which his father had died.

His last conscious words were characteristic of the faith and hope that he always had. When Tom was almost gone, in the hospital, and his brother Fred sought to encourage him with assurances that he'd come through all right, Tom answered, from the subconscious depths of approaching death, "I hope so, I hope so."

His faith might have faltered at times, when things seemed against him, and his spirits were sometimes low — but never for long. And hope he always had, no matter how many and terrible the doubts. This is what he wrote in my presentation copy of "From Death to Morning":

Dear Henry,

I'm a little sad as I write you this. I've just read the first review of this book — in next Saturday's Herald-Tribune — which pans it and sees little in it except a man six foot six creating monstrous figures in a world of five feet eight. — I do not think this is true, but now I have a hunch the well known "reaction" has set in against me, and that I will take a pounding in this book. — Well, I am writing you this because I believe that as good writing as I have ever done is in this book — and because my faith has always been that a good thing is indestructible and that if there is good here — as I hope and believe there is — it will somehow survive. — That is a faith I want to have, and that I think we need in life — and that is why I am writing you this — not in defense against attacks I may receive — but just to put this on record *in advance* with you, who are a friend of mine. — So won't you put this away — what I have written — and keep it — and if someday it turns out I am right — won't you take it out and read it to me?

Yours—

Tom

MY EXPERIENCES WITH THOMAS WOLFE

VARDIS FISHER[1]

On learning that I knew Thomas Wolfe members of his cult — and one runs into them everywhere — invariably ask: "What was he *really* like?" If I give my impression of what he was *really* like they ask, "Why don't you write something about him?" Well, I have had in mind writing something about him for almost ten years now. This impulse in me has always been strongest when I have read something about him written by another. This is true because not only was Wolfe a controversial figure during his last ten years but still is. Almost nobody when viewing Wolfe has been dispassionate. Mr. Herbert J. Muller, author of a study of Thomas Wolfe published in 1947, points out that persons see only his "splendid gifts" or his "shocking sins." Like a certain psychologist they see in him the greatest writer of his time; or they cry impatiently with Bernard DeVoto that genius is not enough, or with W. H. Auden they dismiss his work as so much grandiose rubbish. The blind men are busy with the elephant but Wolfe is not all trunk nor tail nor wall. Though I was fond of him and greatly admire some things in his work I think I can view him without the adulation of his cultists. Though much in his work I simply cannot stand I think I need not fall into the contempt and condescension of his severest critics.

Well, we shall see.

I vividly remember the time I first saw him. In the fall of 1928 I joined the English faculty of Washington Square College in lower Manhattan. About twenty-five or thirty of us occupied one huge room, with desks placed back to back, so that when we sat at our desk we faced a colleague. For some of us four desks were placed in such manner. I sat on the aisle, and Hal White, the poet, was my deskmate at my left. In this room at that time were men — and

[1]Vardis Fisher was Instructor in English at Washington Square College from 1928 to 1931. He is the author of many novels of which the best known are *In Tragic Life* (1932) and *Children of God* (1939).

women — who were later to make names for themselves with one thing or another. A few of them, like Eda Lou Walton, already had names. Among those still to be heard from were Frederic Prokosch, Margaret Schlauch and Edwin Burgum. It was, taken all in all, quite a brilliant English faculty and our departmental head was inordinately proud of it.

One morning, just after the turn of the year, there entered a man who, I observed at once, attracted instant and, in some of his colleagues, critical attention. My back was to the hall doorway and I did not see him when he came in. I did not see him until he strode past me and dropped a pile of books on a desk across the aisle and sank sprawling into a chair. He was so huge, his stride was so long and aggressive, his dark hair was so long and uncombed, his dark eyes were so unhappy and suspicious, and his whole bearing was so obviously that of a man who felt himself called to an uncommon destiny that I stared at him, fascinated. I felt in him then what he was to confess in his books or letters: "By God, I have genius and I shall yet force the inescapable fact down the throats of the rats and vermin who wait the proof." I felt: "Giving my brain and my heart to these stupid little fools; talking like an angel or a God in a language too few of them will understand." I sensed in his whole being his conviction: "There are few heroic lives: about the only one I know a great deal about is my own."

For a few moments I slyly studied the man; when, at last, turning to Hal White I asked in a whisper: "Who is that?" and in a whisper Hal answered, "Tom Wolfe." I had heard the name from our chairman, who had spoken to me about him, saying that at the moment Wolfe was abroad. But I was not prepared for the response of our colleagues. Several of them roundabout were also slyly observing Wolfe and in some of the faces I saw unmistakable distaste.

Seated at my desk I faced uptown. Wolfe, sitting across the aisle and two desks away, faced downtown; and so it was that I had a clear view of him when he sat at his desk and I at mine. I covertly studied him — for without realizing it he invited, almost demanded, attention; and I became aware after a little that Wolfe knew that I was observing him. His face and manner showed it. He resented my furtive but persistent scrutiny but never once did he meet my eyes. It was not his way, I was to learn later, to look anyone straight in the eye. In all my hours with him he never held my gaze for more than a brief moment, and then only to manifest his morbid intolerance of the fixed and searching stare.

He was not often at his desk. It was not his habit, as it was with most of us, to read class papers at his desk or to prepare his lecture notes there or to consult with his students there. Every time he came to his desk I perceived that he was restless, impatient, suspicious, eager to be off. He knew that several of us were interested to discover what manner of man he was, and though no doubt he was flattered he showed only contempt. He had prodigious contempt for pedants, even for college teachers; his contempt for those around him was so plain, yet so childlike in its defensive pose, that I was amused and delighted; and every time he came in I watched him and he knew that I watched him. But he never met my eyes and he never said hello. He never, so far as I observed him, said hello to anyone in that office. He simply strode in, sprawled at his desk and brooded, his eyes flickering with spite, scorn, contempt, malice, anxiety, fear; and after a few minutes he would rise and go away. But again and again I tricked him. I would pretend to be immersed in a book, when, suddenly glancing up, I would surprise him watching me. At once he would look away, and the sardonic distaste in his countenance would become deeper and darker than his own skin.

Well, I knew, of course, that here was an extraordinary person, an extraordinary child, lonely, lost, obsessed, embittered, in the great hulking form of a man. Before I ever exchanged a word with Wolfe I thought I knew a good deal about him. For I was another child, lonely and lost, and I recognized my kin. I also sensed that Wolfe suspected that I was looking more deeply into him than he wanted any man to look.

It was inevitable that he should have come to me at last. I recall that moment. My first novel had been published the previous October. Wolfe's first novel had been accepted by Maxwell Perkins while he was abroad and was to be published this year. He came up to me one day and said briefly and simply, "I read your novel and liked it"— and strode away. But he came again and we became friends, and during the next couple of years we saw a good deal of one another.

Wolfe, whose intuitions were sharp and incisive, recognized in me a kindred spirit. Though my childhood had been spent in a lonely God-forsaken frontier outpost, deep in the west, and his in a city in the east, we had many things in common. I had indeed more in common with him than I have ever had with another friend. We had in common the kind of childhood that had tortured and almost driven us to lunacy; the same lonely introversion of spirit; the same pathetically overdeveloped idealism mingled with deep distrust of human motives; the same monstrous self-pity; the same fright and anxieties; the same kind of identification with the opposite sex and negative ego-identification with father; the same deeply repressed hatred of father; the same problem with women; the same hatred of pretentiousness and sham that sprang largely from an unhappy recognition of sham in ourselves; the same contempt for most human beings, that was only displaced contempt for self — though this I did not know then and I think Wolfe never learned; the same frenzied desire to prove our worth and leave our name on a page of history, though knowing that fame was a bauble and personal immortality the hope of a ravaged soul; the same gross, offensive, and sometimes insufferable egoism that was less egoism than a defense against our overdeveloped submissive tendencies, which in both of us were very strong; the same naked need of spiritual shelters but scorn of formalized religions; and the same tendency to psychic impotence. We were making the same kind of struggle to come out of childhood darkness but I had at that time recognized that the "door" was only a deeper kind of darkness.

We had had — our talks together soon revealed this — the same kind of problems with parents and other relatives. Both had had a dominant and overzealous mother who, though well-meaning and devoted, had never understood her strange child; and the unhappy relationship with mother had colored with unfortunate results our relations with other women. We had had a father who had scared the living daylights out of us, mine with the crude brutalities of the frontier, Wolfe's (these anyway were two) with declamation and fire.

Anyone who would understand Wolfe must understand his relationship with his mother. Mr. Muller, I think, almost entirely missed it. Phallic symbols run through Wolfe's books in teeming numbers, and though Muller alludes to a few of them he apparently did not grasp their significance. In one instance he says that Wolfe's quest of a father "sometimes looks more like the quest of a mother, a yearning for the womb." As though there could be any question about it! He reminds us that Wolfe suckled until he was three and a half years old and slept with his mother until he was a big boy. In a footnote he suggests that Wolfe got the idea "of the search for a father from Maxwell Perkins rather than Joyce"; and a few pages later speaks of "the progress he has made in his search for a father, a door, a home." Door and home have never been with any people, so far as I know, father-symbols: one wonders what the ancient Semitic "door of life" means to Mr. Muller. Why, he asks, was Wolfe such a cad with "Esther," and gives Wolfe's answer, that he returned to the "demon" in man. The demon idea, Muller says, is not "sheer nonsense." It is that and nothing else. Wolfe simply refused to face up to his repressions and went off halfcocked into ancient superstition-symbols. In his early work, Muller points out, Wolfe introduced the theme that he could not go home again, "but by home he means simply Asheville." Subconsciously he did not mean that at all. By home he meant his mother and by his mother he meant the door.

Jung puts it this way: "In order not to be conscious of his desire for incest (his regressive impulse toward animal nature) the son lays the entire blame on the mother, whence results the image of the 'dreaded mother'. 'Mother' becomes a specter of anxiety to him." Wolfe's mother, as anyone can discover by reading his letters to her, became such a specter for Wolfe. "You never write. You never think of me. If I should die here you'd forget me in two months. . . . You don't know me, Mama. I'm not important to you." Again: "I have not yet ceased hoping or believing that there may be left in some of you some genuine atom of affection, sympathy, and good will for me." After all the money she had sent him! Wolfe was sending these reproaches from Europe. He went there year after year for his own profit and pleasure, spending all of his own money on himself, and in letter after letter, year after year, writing to his hard-working and not prosperous mother for money. And she seems to have sent it every time he demanded it. After all, he had slept with her until he was (these are her words) "a great big boy. I kept him a baby." After his curls were cut "the sad part to me — my baby was gone — he was getting away from me." In any case he was trying to. That is why he kept running to Europe. That he was never able to get away from her and then return, as the adult returns, was his tragedy. He writes bitterly from Europe that she has forgotten him and will never see him again; and a few days later she is still sending him money. His self-pitying and petulant ingratitude to his mother makes very painful reading, though we do know of course out of what his ingratitude came.

His problem of his father is just as clear. One day I was with him in that enormous and bleak and ugly room in which he lived for a while, when he did something that astonished me. Scattered over the chairs and floor were books, papers, letters, manuscripts, clothes. We had spent two or three hours together when, called back to our duties, we prepared to leave. Wolfe looked everywhere to be sure that all the cigarettes were out, and I thought at the moment only that his anxiety was extreme. Between thumb and forefinger he crushed them one by one. We then went out and he locked the door but he stood by the door like a man listening to a voice within; when, unlocking the door, he said he would go back to be sure that no cigarette had been left burning. This he did. I concluded then that I was in the presence of a man with a phobia of fire. He came out and locked the door and we descended to the street; and a second time he went back. I was thinking of both of us. My principal phobia had been of water, in which several times when a child I almost drowned.

One of his friends tells me that in his last years he showed no fear of fire, that indeed his desk and some of his papers are cigarette-burned. It may be that my guess was wrong. But if wrong, there was another symbolism present, the nature of which eludes me. I still think that his strange behavior was in some way related to his father. In any case it reveals a great deal about the man, for he was wholly unaware that he was acting abnormally. His almost complete failure to understand the nature and source of the conflicts in him must always be kept in mind by anyone who would understand him.

I never saw him in his last years. In 1939 one of his friends came through Idaho and while we were drinking a cocktail she said, "You knew Wolfe. If he had lived what do you think would have happened to him?" I said I thought he would have gone insane. I thought that because to the day of his death, so far as I know, he had not been able to understand and discipline the tyrannical emotions in him that made him a wanderer among men. His constant wandering is not to be explained by his "great vitality" or his "search for truth." Somewhere he has written, "I feel at times as if I have developed a powerful monster, which will some day destroy me." Muller thinks that before his death "he had indeed made his peace, with his world and with himself." Another friend thinks that he had become quite aware "of the forces inside him" and that this will be proved by his letters to be published soon by Scribner's. I shall remain unconvinced unless the letters show that he had become aware of the nature of his deep and tormenting attachment to his mother and of the reasons why he was a cad with "Esther."

I have said that Wolfe and I talked but that was not the way of it at all. He once wrote his mother that "all of us talk too much." Wolfe talked incessantly and I listened. I had learned that most authors like to talk about themselves, and listen only when they have to and then with obvious impatience. My tolerance was a pose. Now and then Wolfe would ask a question but he seldom gave me a chance to answer it. Now and then he would invite me to speak but always he interrupted me. He had almost no capacity to listen. That was not arrogance on his part. It was fear that he himself had no meaning to communicate or would never be able to make the meaning plain. Hour after hour he poured himself out to me, though here as in his books he never got under the surface to explore his depths.

I recall with not altogether pleasant emotions an evening I spent with him after he had returned from abroad. He told me about his experiences with Sinclair Lewis in England; and I think he had been phrasing the matter over and over in his mind, in the way of writers, because the story as he told it then was much like his account of it which later appeared in one of his novels. That evening, even more than in his published account — for time, I suppose, did something to soften the matter — his contempt for Lewis' histrionics was mad and wicked, though mixed with admiration and compassion.

The thing that had stirred him most deeply, I thought, was his realization that here was a novelist who had just won the highest honor in his field, yet seemed more bedeviled and unhappy than ever, a wanderer in Europe in search of he hardly knew what, and in any case of what he could never hope to find. Wolfe was haunted by the thought that the same sad fate would overtake him if he achieved such wealth and eminence; and he was thrown back again and again to the bitter philosophy of *Ecclesiastes*. "Vanity!" he cried, his lips frothing and slobbering as they always did when he was deeply aroused. "Vanity, it is all vanity!" he howled, with utter contempt for the folly of human striving. But the child in him hoped nevertheless that there was some tower beyond tragedy which

Lewis had not found but which he would find; some nobility in human nature that stood serene and incorruptible above the accursed follies and vanities of egoism; some solace or sanctuary somewhere. His emotions cried for it; his sharp and cynical mind knew that it could not be, at least not in his lifetime, at least not for him.

I speak of his sharp and cynical mind. He had that kind of mind but it looked out of a lonely and adolescent innocence. He had a mind that probed deep into the motives of others and cast a pitiless light over his fellows; but I never felt that he was able to throw that light on himself. If he ever stood revealed to himself in its illumination his books do not show it. Muller speaks again and again of his passionate honesty and sincerity. No man can be honest and sincere without a pretty clear understanding of his own motives and nature. Wolfe the man was the protective and fierce guardian of Wolfe the child that filled the frame of Wolfe the man. The enormity of his blindness to himself, of his self-idolatry, of his frenzied refusal to look at himself for what he was is to be seen in all his novels, but nowhere more painfully than in the first. The most shocking and incredible instance of it, for me, is to be found in the fourth chapter of *Look Homeward, Angel*.

The infant Eugene Gant (Thomas Wolfe) lies in his crib, washed, powdered and fed, and thinking "quietly of many things before he dropped off to sleep." What does the infant Wolfe think about? About the "interminable sleep that obliterated time for him, and that gave him a sense of having missed forever a day of sparkling life." This babe was "heartsick with weary horror as he thought of the discomfort, weakness, dumbness, the infinite misunderstandings he would have to endure before he gained even physical freedom." He grew sick at heart thinking of the long life before him, the "lack of co-ordination of the centers of control, the undisciplined and rowdy bladder . . ." He suffered agonies because he could not talk. He looked at his sniggering relatives round him and "wondered savagely how they would feel if they knew what he really thought"; he had to "laugh at their whole preposterous comedy of errors"; and as they spoke to him words which he did not understand the babe saw that they were mangling them "in the preposterous hope" of making him understand; and "he had to laugh at the fools, in spite of his vexation." And after the relatives went away leaving him in a shuttered room, this infant "saw his life down the solemn vista of a forest aisle, and he knew that he would always be the sad one." He knew that "he must always walk down lonely passages." He "understood that men were forever strangers to one another," that [they are] "imprisoned in the dark womb. . . ." He saw himself as "an inarticulate stranger, an amusing little clown . . ." His "brain went black with terror."

But enough and more than enough. It is the most fantastically silly passage known to me in serious literature — so incredible in its failure to grasp the simplest realities, so painfully maudlin in its glorification of the Wolfe-babe that one doesn't know whether to be more astounded at Wolfe who wrote it or at book reviewers who accepted it as plausible or at Maxwell Perkins who did not throw it out. Perkins has written that he "has plenty of humor when the humor gland is functioning" but the humor gland never functioned when he wrote about himself. As Muller points out, Eugene-Thomas is forever beside himself; he yells, howls, bellows madly, snarls like a wild beast, chokes with fury, turns white with constricted rage or frantic with horror. If he broods it is to contemplate things intolerable, implacable, unutterable. His favorite adjectives are wild, tortured, demented, demonic, maniacal. As Muller says, "extensive quotation is needless and depressing."

Such scenes as the one above offer one clue to Wolfe's personality. He simply gave to the infant the knowledge and perspective, the ironic and malicious reflections of the twenty-seven-year-old man. No other author known to me has so glorified and exalted himself while at the same time using the full power of his faculties to expose other people for what they are. He overcompensated because subconsciously he felt vile and worthless. He made himself his own god. But, as an American psychologist has recently said, talent should not be "used up in defensive distortions of self-healing in a constant kind of self-loving 'artistic' hypochondriasis." He calls attention to the desire too common in artists to exhibit themselves rather than their art. That was Wolfe's fatal defect. As another psychologist puts it, some artists "spend much of their psychic energy maintaining and enhancing their fiction of superiority." If a protest reaction does not set in, "the individual's psychic energy will gradually become wholly directed toward the goal of superiority, he will lose self-perspective and arrive at a manifest egomania." Writing of John Huston, James Agee says: "Huston lacks that deepest kind of creative impulse and that intense self-critical skepticism without which the stature of a great artist is rarely achieved." Intense self-critical skepticism Wolfe did not have.

Picasso has said that an artist paints "to unload himself of feelings and visions." Wolfe once said that an author writes a book to forget it. But he was never able to forget it. He was never able to write out of himself the self-begotten tyrannies and clamorings and proceed to more objective work. He belonged with those persons, among whom Samuel Johnson and Coleridge have been notable instances, whose personality is much bigger than their art. Whether — if he had lived — his personality would eventually have subserved his art nobody, it seems to me, can ever hope to know. But I agree with Muller that emotional maturity would have been the death of him. He was essentially a poet. He had to throw off a million words of slag, among which there would always be a few of unalloyed gold.

Wolfe obsesses Wolfe. Self-pity was the disease in him. There is self-pity in any artist but in Wolfe it was a monstrous tyrant. *That* was the "demon," if Mr. Muller must have a demon. And his self-pity amazed me time and again because when Wolfe looked into another man he looked into his soul. He looked into Sinclair Lewis deeper, it may be, than Lewis has ever looked into himself. Nobody who has read the brilliantly cruel chapters can doubt that he looked to the bottom of Maxwell Perkins. I had no doubt at all that he was looking to the bottom of me. It is, then, all the more astonishing that he was able to turn on himself a reverent gaze that looked through mists and tears.

When reviews of his first book appeared and letters came from his hometown folk his self-pity burst forth in scenes almost too painful to recall. He would come to me with a batch of letters and reviews and he would read them aloud, weeping, cursing, hating — hating as I have never seen a man hate. Sobbing, he would try to get out of himself, to curse out, to vomit out his heartbreak. If it was a critic who had leavened the good black bread of his praise with some yeasty advice Wolfe would gurgle and spit his contempt: "The dull blighted unbuttoned blank-blank!" If it was a letter from his mother, rebuking, exhorting, pleading, scolding he would shake his head sadly and stare down through his tears, saying: "She doesn't understand!" If it was a letter of abuse and threats Wolfe's violent denunciations were unprintable.

I had published a novel and a few of the reviews had stung. An author who says that he is indifferent to reviews of his books, even to reviews by obvious fools, is I am sure self-deceived or lying. Our skins are not thick. Stupid or malicious reviews do hurt. But I would have thought myself an awful ass to weep over them or to allow them to squander my energy. Muller gives that famous passage in which "a huge, naked, intolerable shame and horror pressed on Eugene . . . crushing and palpable like wet gray skies of autumn . . . hideous gray stuff filled him from brain to bowels . . . a naked stare from walls and houses . . . tasted it on his lips, endured it in the screaming and sickening dissonance of ten thousand writing nerves . . exhaustion . . . wild unrest. . . . He saw the whole earth with sick eyes, sick heart, sick flesh . . . writhing nerves of this gray accursed weight of shame and horror . . . he could not die but must live hideously . . . forever in a state of retching and abominable nausea of heart, brain, bowels, flesh and spirit. . . ." And why? Because Eugene had just received his first rejection slip!

I felt deeply sorry for Wolfe, for I knew how he suffered; but I was amazed by the way he exploded, wept and cursed. There he sat, his cheeks bathed, his eyes evil with contempt and hate and hurt, his loose wet lips pouring upon the "rats and vermin" all the vials of his wrath. "They all hate me," he said, "but I must go on! Vardis, we must go on! Don't ever let the low stinking blank-blanks stop you!" He used a telling expression that he was to use again and again: "They're so damned little that they smell little!" His hurt was the more absurd because on all his books he got a good press, even, with few exceptions, an effusively enthusiastic press.

What a man! What a lost and suffering child! When I was a lad my mother, too busy to be a mother herself, forced me to be parents, guardian, protector and spiritual adviser to my brother who, having at that time a physical defect, was the victim everywhere of the bully boys. The urge to protect the weak, the crippled, the helpless was hugely overdeveloped in me. I wanted to go out and thresh Wolfe's "enemies" one by one. I see again his hands folding, crushing, destroying the offensive review or letter; his great shoulders hunched forward; his loose wet mouth, the mouth of the child, the orphan — lost, O lost! — lost to his people, to life, lost above all to himself; lost to the perspective and discipline which any artist must have; lost to that vigilant oversight without which the artist is the victim of his own spiritual corrosions and tyrannies. I still see those dark hurt eyes, wet and wicked, flickering with malice and spite; I can still feel his hot lusting for vengeance. He never forgot what he took to be a slight or a meanness and he never forgave it.

To his mother he wrote: "It has taken me twenty-seven years to rise above the bitterness and hatred of my childhood." He had not risen above it. He hated with a depth and fixedness of purpose which I have never found in another person. One of his friends says, "You are dead right about the young Wolfe hating everything, but he didn't do this so much later when he was surer of himself." In the years when I knew him his hate was never focused and directed, never selective, and as a consequence it wore him out. He simply hated around him in all directions, and there were times — I knew this well — when he hated me. He adopted me, as he was to adopt Perkins, as a kind of mother — *not father, but mother.* His strong feminine nature made that inevitable. I knew the few times he sought me out that he felt a need of me, of what seemed to him to be, but heavens knows was not, my cool and well-disciplined inner core. I suppose I seemed to be quite austere, poised, at ease. Possibly for him I seemed to be one who had found the Jeffers tower beyond tragedy. But I had sense enough to realize that if I were with him too much our friendship would not endure. His affective tolerance was very restricted.

His overdeveloped submissive tendencies had created in him a much greater need to give than to receive. Because of this, he was afraid of those toward whom he felt a strong urge to yield. He felt — subconsciously, of course: if it had been conscious he would not have had the problem — that if he went very far in giving, or *too far,* he would lose his individuality. That subconscious fear is likely to be present in anyone, man or woman, whose overidentification with the opposite sex is tied up with overdevelopment of the sub-missive tendencies. I speak as one of them, though this in me I had not realized when I knew Wolfe. That in Wolfe explains why he could not be, why he dared not be, the lover of any woman very long. That, to anticipate, is the chief reason he left Perkins, whose nature also was strangely feminine. I have known only a few of Wolfe's friends but I should imagine that the women in their na-ture were quite masculine, that the men, like Perkins and me, were quite feminine, not in appearance with either men or women but in personality, interests, intuitions, tastes. Those labor in vain who would understand the artist without recognizing this fundamental truth. Most of the stuff about Hemingway is an astonishing instance of what I mean.

Wolfe's feminine nature was so strong — with *his* childhood how could it have been otherwise? — that he was subconsciously tortured by the threat of capitulation. It is this that made his egoism seem at times to be so enormous and offensive: *that* was only a defense against absorption of self by life, or, more narrowly, by people, such as mistresses with masculine strivings, toward whom such men when unaware of their nature are inevitably drawn; and toward editors with contempt for women, whose own essentially feminine outlook aggravated Wolfe's deep anxieties, and heaped futility upon his efforts to find his maleness.

I early recognized some of these things in Wolfe. Or possibly I should say that I sensed them, sensed that his overpowering egoism was a defense against over submissiveness; that his fear of women grew out of the fact that he was too much woman himself; that his terrors and self-pity and overdramatizations were nourished by a disordered and unintegrated personality. I sensed them because these things were also in me and I was trying to understand them. I was careful to let him feel that I would put no demands on his precarious and almost tentative sense of self-adequacy. Wolfe could be held, if held at all, as friend or lover only by letting him back away when he felt stifled by his deep and abiding yearning to lay his heart at somebody's feet and his soul with it.

One of the psychologists alluded to above, Daniel E. Schneider in *The Psychoanalyst and the Artist,* thinks that Wolfe was possibly the greatest American writer of his time but that "lyrical overplay" destroyed form in his work; and that without "monumental editorial help" it is doubtful that his work would have appeared in the form in which it appeared. Coming from a psychologist writing about the artist, both statements seem to me to be pretty thin. Wolfe's work does not have much form; his editor selected and rearranged the materials within the loose frame of the autobiographical chronicle. The lyrical overplay was the essence of Wolfe, the poet, and far from destroying form gave to his stories a kind of lyrical continuity. All his work lies in the pattern of the lineal flow of time and the river.

How important he was as a writer I do not pretend to know. No one with tolerance for the brasses and cymbals in the music of human emotion can fail enormously to enjoy many of Wolfe's scenes. My tolerance is restricted for exaggeration, emotional excesses, and blacks and whites in character delineation. Auden says he had a "false conception of human nature" but Muller reminds his readers that after experimenting with various modern faiths, Auden "has returned to the doctrine of Original Sin!" Muller points out what needs no pointing out for enlightened minds, that the notion of original sin is "as false to the actual complexities and paradoxes" of life as the opposite view of natural goodness. But it is true that in Wolfe's books people are awfully good, like Eugene most of the time, or awfully bad, like most of the others. Such a view is false.

Clifton Fadiman has said that Wolfe had the greatest command of language of any author of his time. On the contrary, language was in command of him. To one thing and to one alone did he give himself fully — not to food or drink or women or friendship, no, but to words. He suffered from overpraise. Canby says, for instance, that *no scene* in *You Can't Go Home Again* could have been equalled by any other living writer. It is true that Wolfe had enormous talent for creating profane, vulgar, rowdy, boisterous scenes in which most of the characters are heels. But he overdid it. His talent in character was that of caricature. His talent in scene was "romantic." His talent in language was too largely an undiscriminating engulfing of Roget.

Muller thinks he came close to the creation of the American myth. He had the talent for it. Like his country, he grossly and lustily exaggerated everything, including his lovemaking, hungers, strivings, torments, ambitions and plans. His cultists were busy before he died converting him into a stupendous legend. In a little book that I have prepared on writing I put it this way:

"He was, of course, the kind of man who is born and built for the mythmakers. Too huge for ordinary beds or clothes or automobiles, too tall for ordinary windows and doors, he came on the American scene with a book to match his size; and Americans, with their interest in bigness of all kinds, took him to their hearts. With the publication of his first book the myth started, and he pitched in to help it grow. One of the themes running through his volumes is to be found in the word devour. At once the Wolfe protagonist began to devour everything in sight — books, food, women, drink, far places, and everything else that a titan could possibly feed on. Everything from then on was oversized, and from wonder to wonder the size grew. Little men gazed upon him with rapturous astonishment. Little women placed themselves in the way of easy capture. And he took everything as his right. He was becoming a legend and to fertilize the legend he made his manuscripts bigger and bigger; and the mythmakers got busy with these also, spreading the story that they were delivered by truck in enormous bales. Wolfe tried to become a symbol of what he thought was his country's meaning. I sat with him one morning at breakfast and he devoured enough for ten men. He wolfed it down, to use another of his favorite words; but in observing him closely I was not at all persuaded that he was conscious of eating. He was simply taken over body and soul by the job of being big.

"That is all right but for the fact that Wolfe was being defeated by the myth. If he had lived it would have been fascinating to watch the labors of the mythmakers as the myth developed. The myth was engulfing him and in trying to fill its stupendous vacuum he was losing sight of the man. He was in danger of losing sight of life itself and passing off into the stratosphere like a wandering nebula. Because the mythmakers destroy what they build, as in all times past they destroyed their gods. The thing created is at last engulfed by its overzealous creators. In ancient times people ate their gods, and, later, their god-surrogates, such as the bull and lamb; and today they create the myth-god only to devour it. It takes an artist of tough fiber to develop in his votaries a case of indigestion. . . ."

I showed those words to one of Wolfe's friends and got my knuckles rapped. The friend says he did not fertilize the legend. But what does Perkins say? "He seems to feel a certain shame at the idea of turning out a book of reasonable dimensions." Edward C. Aswell has confessed that he made three books out of a pile of manuscript "eight feet high." If we allow two inches to the ream there must have been 20,000 pages there!

He was trying to create the American myth and very possibly he did have the talent for it if that talent could have been disciplined and directed; but as things turned out he is for me one of the American tragedies of our time. He is a tragedy in a country whose romantic excesses suffocate its sense of the realities; whose love of freedom is less than its love of power; whose devotion to duty is less than its devotion to self-righteousness; and whose whole notion of truth is Paul's rather than the Preacher's. Among so much that is superficial and shoddy Wolfe was never able to find his bearings; and, rebelling against the cynical wisdom and weariness of such men as Perkins, he fled into the adolescent cloudland of apostrophe. Those who would know some of the best and much of the worst in what Muller calls the American myth can turn to his books, for better than any other writer he set it down. In the last chapters of *You Can't Go Home Again* they will find the callow and sentimental worst, until they come to the last six lines, when they will find this land and this writer at their magnificent best.

I never saw Wolfe after 1931. He was then going abroad and I was returning to the west. He put out a hand to clasp mine and said, "Vardis, don't let the blankety-blank sons of blank lick you. Keep fighting, God damn it . . ." When he turned away his eyes were wet.

In the year of his death he came west and in Boise tried to find me but failed. He spread legends as he journeyed, spawned by his own fertile fancy. He told, for instance (the story has come to me from Santa Fe, Salt Lake City and Portland), that when we were teaching colleagues we got as drunk as owls to screw up the courage to face our classes. We were never drunk together. I suspect I know what gave him the idea for that legend.

It is true that we were afraid to meet our classes, that we recoiled from the cynical faces and ineducable minds of some of our students.

Anxiety arouses tension in the bladder. One afternoon, when we both had classes on the same hall at the same hour, we appeared before the closed doors and paused there. Each knew, with a sense of ironic delight, why the other hesitated. I went to the men's room to void when there was no need and came out and disappeared down the hall but not into my classroom. I spied on Wolfe and in a few moments he vanished into the men's room. I hastened in after him and stood, watching and listening, when suddenly he swung and looked at me and our eyes met. We both understood. We faced one another with the same silly self-conscious smile.

It was in such moments that I loved Wolfe best, for then the child stood forth, naked and defenseless. It is in such moments that I like to remember him.

REPLACING TOM WOLFE

RUSSELL KRAUSS[1]

Returning from Europe in the fall of 1929, just in time to be engulfed in the maelstrom of panic, I began applying with frantic insistency to Dr. Homer A. Watt for a place — any place, even a part-time teaching fellowship — in his department. Dr. Watt already knew me from an earlier encounter, and, though still a bit piqued at my having previously thrown up a fellowship of his procuring, he now agreed to keep me in mind as of possible use in an emergency — unlikely, however, to occur (he warned) since men were beginning to hold to jobs with new tenacity of fear. But despite wanhope, about the middle of January, 1930, I received a hurried summons from Dr. Watt. The unlooked-for emergency had occurred: On the strength of the reception of *Look Homeward, Angel*, Scribner's had offered Tom Wolfe an advance ($2500, I understood), over and above current royalties, provided he give up teaching and devote all his time to writing. I was to take Wolfe's place at Washington Square.

I was not unduly impressed at the honor or privilege of following Wolfe. I had not yet read his book; I had no prescience of the near idolatry to be accorded him in the future; being only twenty-six, I had not yet accepted the dictate of destiny or irresolution which closed to me the path by which he was to reach the heights; besides, by a combination of circumstance and good fortune, I had for some years been wading hip deep in authors already assured of fame. I had met, seen, spoken to — come in contact with in some way, chiefly at Oxford or in Paris — Hemingway, Nathan and Sholem Asch, Gertrude Stein, Harold Stearns, Ford Madox Ford, James Joyce, John Drinkwater, John Masefield, Robert Bridges, John Gould Fletcher, Ezra Pound, Sinclair Lewis, and a dozen others. There was in me no proper awe. As for Wolfe himself, I had met

[1]Former Penfield Fellow and Instructor in English at New York University, Dr. Russell Krauss is now Professor of English in New Jersey State Teachers College, Montclair, New Jersey.

(just *met*) him through his colleague and fellow novelist at the Square, my longtime friend, Vardis Fisher. Publishing almost simultaneously in the fall of 1929 — Fisher's book was the first installment of his *In Tragic Life* tetralogy — the two young authors had, as I recall, exchanged presentation copies of their books. It was to Vardis I therefore went to borrow *Look Homeward, Angel*, feeling that I ought to brief myself as successor, in a sense, to its author. Vardis admitted to me with a rival's grudge that the book had merits, especially in its descriptions of food and the partaking thereof. But he confided his opinion that Wolfe would prove a one-book man, having written himself out autobiographically up practically to the day of publication. A few days later, Wolfe expressed to me an almost identical opinion of Vardis and his book. Fisher's book, as Wolfe apparently did not then know, was his fourth (including a volume of sonnets) to be published and at least the seventh of his writing; none of us, of course, yet knew what monumental chiseling Maxwell Perkins had already performed on the Rushmore of Tom Wolfe.

At the time of my taking over, Wolfe was teaching two sections of freshman composition and two of sophomore survey of English and American literature, one of each in the morning at the School of Fine Arts and another of each in the afternoon at Washington Square College. I seem to remember that his days were Monday, Wednesday and Friday though they could have followed some other pattern. Until the other day, when, in the interest of accuracy, I searched out such records as I have preserved (more or less by accident), I had always carried in memory the belief that the morning classes I inherited from him were under the sponsorship of the School of *Architecture,* dean of which was Professor Bossange. But my old contract with NYU, drawn up in March, 1930, predated to February 1, of the same year, charges half my salary against the School of *Fine Arts*, of which, evidently, *Architecture* is — or then was — a division. The School of Architecture (or Fine Arts) had not yet, in the closing days of Wolfe's tenure there, moved to the Crystal Building though it did do so at about the moment I actually assumed his classes. Momentarily this School was poised in a loft just off Fifth Avenue, in the Thirties, on your right as you face north, not far from B. Altman's. The ground floor was occupied by a Schrafft's unit. I remember something of the location, of the bleakness of the draughting rooms, of the drab layout and furnishment of Wolfe's classroom (undoubtedly used also by other teachers of "academic" subjects, borrowed from Washington Square) — and I remember vaguely the Schrafft's.

At the time of my succeeding Wolfe, though I was his junior by several years, I had, nevertheless, had roughly three years' experience as a college instructor of English. Furthermore, I had taught Latin and philosophy as an undergraduate fellow at the University of Utah; and, what I then regarded as the capstone of a distinguished career, I was just back from a full year of teaching, on the Floating University (around the world), nearly every college subject that can be handled by way of linguistic or semantic approach. Even now, in the mature judgment of my years, I would venture the supposition that I was then at least as qualified as Wolfe, however I might fail to match him otherwise, to take over a simple assignment in freshman composition and sophomore survey. He insisted, nonetheless, that for me to get the hang of what he was doing and had intended afterwards to do, and for him to protect his abandoned flock from lapse and its consequences, I should attend his classes and observe him and his methods for as many of his remaining sessions as possible. Since not awe nor veneration could have dictated abnegation in me, I can only presume at this distance of time that the shocked condition in which so many jobless found themselves in those days motivated my lamblike acquiescence. I have never really cared to observe the teaching methods of any teachers, nor to have my own, if I have any, "observed."

My memory of what followed Wolfe's seignorial summons to me is that, manfully, on some three (or perhaps, four,) mornings, I met him at the shambles then serving as quarters for a great school of

148

architecture. There on each occasion, after, on the first one, having been introduced down the rollbook alphabetically to each student, I sat at an unoccupied desk in the rear of the room and "observed" drowsily through an uninspired hour. (I here note, parenthetically, that I have never of late years met and discoursed with a *literate* former student of Tom Wolfe's who did not recall, from long ago, sessions of wonder to recite as vividly and circumstantially as did "Apollodorus, who repeats to his companion the dialogue which he had heard from Aristodemus, and had already once narrated to Glaucon" though the matter was of some twenty years since. The difficulty with using *illiterate* ex-students of the same Wolfe as a scientific Arrowsmithian control is that so few of them seem to remember who, despite his height, taught them their freshman English.) After the first class, on each day that I attended, Wolfe and I descended to the Schrafft's on the ground floor. There was a gap of an hour between his two classes and invariably he spent that hour drinking black coffee out of a Swedish cup holding at least an imperial pint. (At his request to the staff I got coffee with cream and sugar out of a conventional Schrafft cup of commercial capacity.) The waitresses, blooming expectancy, were ready for Wolfe when he came down. The coffee, which they brought to him in a grey-galvanized gallon picnic pot, was quite obviously the drawn-off dregs of the morning breakfast make; the coffee steward was already cleaning the great brownish cloth filters and setting up the machines for the noonday brew. There was no evidence on the three or four occasions when I accompanied him to the restaurant that Wolfe paid for his coffee or was expected to do so. Neither did he tip the waitresses in my presence; I do not think he recompensed them at all — they seemed his Marthas. After coffee I attended each time his second class. I do not remember at this late date whether composition came before survey, or vice versa.

What I do remember is that the morning sessions sated me; I always contrived some waylayance to my arriving at Washington Square for possible assistance at a further seance in the afternoon.

But considering the experiences of Eugene Gant and George Webber with the female segment of the undergraduate population of the "School for Utility Cultures" and considering the stunned adoration of Schrafft's waitresses of which I was witness, I can only regret that I then possessed so little psychological curiosity as to shirk attendance at those afternoon co-educational gatherings at Washington Square; there were no women, then at least, in the School of Architecture. I remember further that one morning Wolfe's actual stint in English 35 (sophomore survey), it could have been justified as germane, but likewise in English 1 (freshman composition), where justifying it would have required some sophisticating, was a Whitmanesque oral rendering of Ben Jonson's "To the Memory of My Beloved Master, William Shakespeare." He followed each such assault on his captive audience with the vehement affirmation: "God! men, that is poetry! That *is poetry!*" The students, some of them, later told me that on what they dubbed "bad days" Ben Jonson and his elegy rather frequently made up the substance of a class (for English 35 Wolfe used Watt and Munn, *Ideas and Forms in English and American Literature*, a text which tolerates some departures from the strict chronological approach). I have never, myself, even with lingering commentary, been able to stretch Jonson's poem to a full hour's coverage.

During the season of his withdrawing and for a brief spell thereafter, Wolfe from time to time bade me to his apartment, from front to back of a brownstone on 16th Street, where, if it was day and bright, "Mrs. Esther Jack" with her assistant (as I presume) went on with their work at the draughting tables before the wide windows, ignoring our presence except for initial salutation. With what I then no doubt considered sophistication and savoir faire, I accepted her being there as normal domestic oddity. So I came to know nothing about her, really, until *You Can't Go Home Again* introduced her to me as a projection of pure imagination. At Wolfe's foul lodgings I saw the now-much-reported-upon hat boxes full of undecipherable manuscript on every type of paper, including butcher's wrapping, shoved under a crumpled grey-sheeted bed into a warm nest of dust kittens. I handled personally the fabled cigar boxes of pencil butts with which he thumbed his scrawlings. I refused coffee from the pot in which superimposed grounds accumulated until there was no more room for the liquid brew. In a corner on the floor I viewed with mine own eyes the heap of putrid white shirts from which from time to time he would re-select for current wear the one to him least dirty and wrinkled, but to the neutral observer hardly selectable. There in the stinking lair that was his home, he would brief me on individual recalcitrants and recusants among his pupils, subjecting them *in absentia* to Freudian and Adlerian analysis. I could not decide in those days whether he was truly concerned for my understanding of them and my sympathy toward them as new soft charges or whether he was just parsing himself a new character in his next book.

Wolfe's last professional communication with me, if I can trust the surviving records, was a note he left for me on his former desk (now mine as accessory to the job I took from him) in the English Department office — then second floor, Main — at Washington Square College. The note was about delinquent grades:

"Dear Mr. Krauss: All the grades are now in — I just took the Eng. 35 — Thursday night set — upstairs. They were pretty bad — *9 F's*, including several who did not take the final examination; about *14 D's*; *5 C's* and *2 B's*. Even so, I was probably generous.

"I read over the term papers at the same time I read the final exams: I am still putting comments on them and will give them to you early next week. I hope to see you again to give you any information that might be useful.

"With best wishes for good luck and success,

Faithfully yours,
Thomas Wolfe
Friday, Feb. 7.

"I'll also give you the grade books next week.

"The English 35 final exams, together with the term quizzes, are in your upper left hand desk drawer."

Perhaps it was the spirit as exhibited in this note that accounted for what seemed at the time an unwarranted, since I was unknown as yet to them, personal tribute in the warmth of the welcome which my new pupils extended to me. Wolfe kept back his survey text, as inscribed by Dr. Watt, but he turned over to me his book of freshman readings, *Literary Studies for Freshman Composition,* which I still possess. In this latter there are random jottings and some pencilled theme suggestions, not above the uninspired level with which we professorial robots are content — for instance "The Five Minutes When I Thought I Was Dying."

BIBLIOGRAPHY

I · BOOKS BY THOMAS WOLFE

Look Homeward, Angel. New York: Charles Scribner's Sons, 1929.

Of Time and the River. New York: Charles Scribner's Sons, 1935.

From Death to Morning. New York: Charles Scribner's Sons, 1935.

The Story of a Novel. New York: Charles Scribner's Sons, 1936.

The Web and the Rock. New York: Harper and Brothers, 1939.

A Note on Experts: Dexter Vespasian Joyner. New York: House of Books, 1939.

The Face of a Nation (poetical passages from the writings . . . selected by John Hall Wheelock). New York: Harper and Brothers, 1939.

You Can't Go Home Again. New York: Harper and Brothers, 1940.

Gentlemen of the Press, A Play. Chicago: Black Archer, 1942.

The Hills Beyond (with a Note on Thomas Wolfe by Edward C. Aswell). New York: Harper and Brothers, 1943.

Thomas Wolfe's Letters to His Mother, edited with an Introduction by John Skally Terry. New York: Charles Scribner's Sons, 1943.

A Stone, A Leaf, A Door (selected and arranged in verse by John S. Barnes). New York: Charles Scribner's Sons, 1945.

The Portable Thomas Wolfe, ed. Maxwell Geismar. New York: Viking Press, 1946.

Mannerhouse. New York: Harper and Brothers, 1948.

The Years of Wandering in Many Lands and Cities. New York: C. S. Boesen, 1949.

Western Journal. Pittsburgh: University of Pittsburgh, 1951.

153

II · BOOKS ABOUT WOLFE

Adams, Agatha Boyd. *Thomas Wolfe: Carolina Student* ("Extension Publication," Vol. XV, No. 2, January 1950). Chapel Hill: University of North Carolina Library, 1950.

Basso, Hamilton. "Thomas Wolfe," *After the Genteel Tradition*, ed. Malcolm Cowley. New York: W. W. Norton and Company, 1937.

Beach, Joseph Warren. *American Fiction: 1920-1940*. New York: The Macmillan Company, 1941.

Bernstein, Aline Frankau. *Three Blue Suits*. New York: Equinox House, 1935.

————. *The Journey Down*. New York: Alfred A. Knopf, 1938.

————. *An Actor's Daughter*. New York: Alfred A. Knopf, 1941.

————. *Miss Condon*. New York: Alfred A. Knopf, 1947.

Brodin, Pierre. *Thomas Wolfe*. Asheville, N.C.: Stephens Press, 1949.

Burlingame, Roger. *Of the Making of Many Books: A Hundred Years of Reading, Writing, and Publishing*. New York: Charles Scribner's Sons, 1946.

Daniels, Jonathan W. *Tar Heels: A Portrait of North Carolina*. New York: Dodd, Mead and Company, 1941. ["Poet of the Boom" is also in *The Enigma of Thomas Wolfe*, pp. 77-90.]

Delakas, Daniel L. *Thomas Wolfe, la France, et les romanciers français*. Paris: Jouve, 1950.

Geismar, Maxwell. *Writers in Crisis: The American Novel Between Two Wars*. Boston: Houghton Mifflin Company, 1942. ["Diary of a Provincial" is also in *The Enigma of Thomas Wolfe*, pp. 109-19.]

Gelfant, Blanche. "Urbanization as an Influence on Dreiser, Dos Passos, and Wolfe." Unpublished Doctor's thesis, University of Wisconsin, 1948.

Hodgin, David R. *The Ballad of Tall Tom Wolfe*. Asheville, N.C.: Stephens Press, 1949.

154

Johnson, Pamela Hansford. *Hungry Gulliver, an English Critical Appraisal.* New York: Charles Scribner's Sons, 1948.

Kazin, Alfred. *On Native Grounds: An Interpretation of Modern American Prose Fiction.* New York: Reynal and Hitchcock, 1942.

McCoy, Lola L. *Tom Wolfe's "Dixieland."* Asheville, N.C.: Thomas Wolfe Memorial Association, 1949.

McCormick, John O. "The Novels of Thomas Wolfe." Unpublished Doctor's thesis, Yale University, 1948.

Muller, Herbert Joseph. *Thomas Wolfe.* Norfolk, Conn.: New Directions, 1947.

Norwood, Hayden. *The Marble Man's Wife, Thomas Wolfe's Mother.* New York: Charles Scribner's Sons, 1947.

Perkins, Maxwell. "Scribner's and Tom Wolfe," *The Enigma of Thomas Wolfe,* ed. Richard Walser. Cambridge: Harvard University Press, 1953.

[Perkins, Maxwell.] *Editor to Author: The Letters of Maxwell Perkins,* (selected and edited, with commentary and an Introduction, by John Hall Wheelock). New York: Charles Scribner's Sons, 1950.

Preston, George R., Jr. *Thomas Wolfe: A Bibliography.* New York: C. S. Boesen, 1943.

Rothman, Nathan L. "Thomas Wolfe and James Joyce," *A Southern Vanguard,* ed. Allen Tate. New York: Prentice-Hall, Inc., 1947. [Also in *The Enigma of Thomas Wolfe,* pp. 263-89.]

Smith, E. G. M. *Wolfe's Unfinished Symphony.* Unpublished Doctor's thesis, University of Wisconsin, 1948.

Walser, Richard, ed. *The Enigma of Thomas Wolfe: Biographical and Critical Selections.* Cambridge: Harvard University Press, 1953.

III · PERIODICAL ARTICLES ABOUT WOLFE

Albrecht, W. P. "Time as Unity in Thomas Wolfe," *New Mexico Quarterly Review*, XIX (Autumn 1949), 320-29. [Also in *The Enigma of Thomas Wolfe*, pp. 239-48.]

————. "The Title of *Look Homeward, Angel*," *Modern Language Quarterly*, XI (March 1950), 50-57.

Allen, Lee. "Tom Wolfe," *American Mercury*, LXIV (March 1947), 381.

Ames, R. S. "Wolfe, Wolfe!," *American Spectator*, III (January 1935), 5-6.

Armstrong, Anne W. "As I Saw Thomas Wolfe," *Arizona Quarterly*, II (Spring 1946), 5-14.

Askew, Ruth. "The Harp of Death for Thomas Wolfe," *Southwest Review*, XXXIII (Autumn 1948), 348.

Aswell, E. C. "Thomas Wolfe Did Not Kill Maxwell Perkins," *The Saturday Review of Literature*, XXXIV (October 6, 1951), 16-17.

————; J. S. Terry. "En route to a Legend: Two Interpretations," *The Saturday Review of Literature*, XXXI (November 27, 1948), 7-9; 7, 34-36. [The first in *The Enigma of Thomas Wolfe*, pp. 51-63, under Terry's name and the title "Wolfe and Perkins."]

Baker, Carlos. "Thomas Wolfe's Apprenticeship," *Delphian Quarterly*, XXIII (January 1940), 20-25.

Basso, Hamilton. "Thomas Wolfe: A Portrait," *New Republic*, LXXVII (June 24, 1936), 199-202.

————. "Thomas Wolfe: A Summing Up," *New Republic*, CIII (September 23, 1940), 422-23.

Bates, E. S. "Thomas Wolfe," *English Journal*, XXVI (September 1937), 519-27.

————. "Thomas Wolfe," *Modern Quarterly*, XI (Fall 1938), 86-88.

Bishop, J. P. "The Sorrows of Thomas Wolfe," *The Kenyon Review*, I (Winter 1939), 7-17.

Blythe, Le Gette. "The Thomas Wolfe I Knew," *The Saturday Review of Literature*, XXVIII (August 25, 1945), 18-19.

Braswell, William. "Thomas Wolfe Lectures and Takes a Holiday," *College English*, I (October 1939), 11-22. [Also in *The Enigma of Thomas Wolfe*, pp. 64-76.]

Bridges, A. P. "Thomas Wolfe: Legends of a Man's Hunger for His Youth," *The Saturday Review of Literature*, XI (April 6, 1935), 599, 609.

Brown, E. K. "Thomas Wolfe: Realist and Symbolist," *University of Toronto Quarterly*, X (January 1941), 153-66. [Also in *The Enigma of Thomas Wolfe*, pp. 206-21.]

Burgum, E. B. "Thomas Wolfe's Discovery of America," *Virginia Quarterly Review*, XXII (June 1946), 421-37. [Also in *The Enigma of Thomas Wolfe*, 179-94.]

Burt, Struthers. "Catalyst for Genius: Maxwell Perkins, 1884-1947," *The Saturday Review of Literature*, XXXIV (June 9, 1951), 6-8, 36-39.

Cargill, Oscar. "Gargantua Fills His Skin," *University of Kansas City Review*, XVI (Autumn 1949), 20-30.

Carpenter, F. I. "Thomas Wolfe: The Autobiography of an Idea," *University of Kansas City Review*, XII (Summer 1946), 179-88.

Church, Margaret. "Thomas Wolfe: Dark Time," *PMLA*, LXIV (September 1949), 628-38. [Also in *The Enigma of Thomas Wolfe*, pp. 249-62.]

Collins, T. L. "Thomas Wolfe," *Sewanee Review*, L (October-December 1942), 487-504. [Also in *The Enigma of Thomas Wolfe*, pp. 161-78.]

Colum, Mary. "Limits of Thomas Wolfe," *Forum*, CII (November 1939), 227.

Cowley, Malcolm. "Maxwell Perkins" [profile], *The New Yorker*, April 8, 1944, pp. 30-43.

———. "Thomas Wolfe's Legacy," *New Republic*, XCIX (July 19, 1939), 311-12.

————. "Wolfe and the Lost People," *New Republic*, CV (November 3, 1941), 592-94.

Cross, Neal. "Thomas Wolfe: If I Am Not Better," *Pacific Spectator*, IV, No. 4 (1950), 488-96.

Cummings, R. [and others]. "Wolfe and Perkins" [letters], *The Saturday Review of Literature*, XXXIV (August 11, 1951), 22-25.

Daniels, Jonathan. "Thomas Wolfe," *The Saturday Review of Literature*, XIII (September 24, 1938), 3-4.

Davis, Ruth. "Look Homeward, Angel" [transcript of talk given by Mrs. Julia Elizabeth Wolfe to New York University class, November 30, 1935], *The Saturday Review of Literature*, XXIX (January 5, 1946), 13-14, 31-32.

Delakas, Daniel. "L'Expérience français de Thomas Wolfe," *Revue de littérature comparée*, XXIV (July-September, 1950), 417-36.

Ehrsam, T. G. "I Knew Thomas Wolfe," *Book Collector's Journal*, I (June 1936), 1, 3. [Digested in *Fact Digest*, V (March 1938), 14-17.]

Falk, Robert. "Thomas Wolfe and the Critics," *College English*, V (January 1944), 186-92.

Figueira, Gastón. "Poetas y prosistas americanos: I. Edwin Arlington Robinson. II. Thomas Wolfe," *Revista iberoamericana*, XI (October 1946), 329-32.

Fisher, Vardis. "My Experiences with Thomas Wolfe," *Tomorrow*, X (April 1951), 24-30.

————. "Thomas Wolfe — Maxwell Perkins," *Tomorrow*, X (July 1951), 20-25.

Frohock, W. M. "Thomas Wolfe: Of Time and Neurosis," *Southwest Review*, XXXIII (Autumn 1938), 349-60. [Also in *The Enigma of Thomas Wolfe*, pp. 222-38.]

Geismar, Maxwell. "Thomas Wolfe: The Hillman and the Furies," *Yale Review*, XXXV (N.S.) (June 1946), 649-65.

Glicksberg, C. I. "Thomas Wolfe," *Canadian Forum*, XV (January 1936), 24-25.

Haugen, Einar. "Thomas Wolfes siste bok," *Samtiden* [Oslo], LV (1946), 641-45.

Heiderstadt, Dorothy. "Studying Under Thomas Wolfe," *Mark Twain Quarterly*, VIII (Winter 1950), 7-8.

Hutsell, James K. "As They Recall Thomas Wolfe," *Southern Packet*, IV (April 1948), 4, 9-10.

————. "Thomas Wolfe and 'Altamont,'" *Southern Packet*, IV (April 1948), 1-4.

Jack, P. M. "Remembering Thomas Wolfe," *The New York Times Book Review*, October 2, 1938, pp. 2, 28.

Jaffard, Paul. "L'Oeuvre de Thomas Wolfe," *Critique* [France], VII (August-September 1951), 686-93.

Jones, H. M. "Thomas Wolfe's Short Stories," *The Saturday Review of Literature*, XIII (November 30, 1935), 13.

Kauffman, Bernice. "Bibliography of Periodical Articles on Thomas Wolfe," *Bulletin of Bibliography*, XVII (May 1942), 162-65 and (August 1942) 172-90.

Kazin, Alfred. "Chiel Takin' Notes," *New Republic*, CVIII (May 3, 1943), 607-9.

Kennedy, Richard S. "Thomas Wolfe at Harvard, 1920-1923," *Harvard Library Bulletin*, IV (Spring 1950), 172-90 and (Autumn 1950) 304-19. [Also in *The Enigma of Thomas Wolfe*, pp. 18-32.]

Kohler, Dayton. "Thomas Wolfe: Prodigal and Lost," *College English*, I (October 1939), 1-10.

Kreymborg, Alfred. "Thomas Wolfe, Poet," *The Saturday Review of Literature*, XXVIII (November 3, 1943), 32.

Kronenberger, Louis. "Thomas Wolfe, Autobiographer," *The Nation*, CXLIX (July 15, 1939), 75-76.

Kussy, Bella. "The Vitalist Trend in Thomas Wolfe," *Sewanee Review*, L (July-September 1942), 306-23.

159

Ledwig-Rowohlt, H. M. "Thomas Wolfe in Berlin," *American Scholar*, XXII (Spring 1953), 185-201.

Little, Thomas. "The Thomas Wolfe Collection of William B. Wisdom," *Harvard Library Bulletin*, I (Autumn 1947), 280-88.

Macauley, Thurston. "Thomas Wolfe: A Writer's Problems," *Publishers' Weekly*, CXXXIV (December 24, 1938), 2150-52.

McCole, C. J. "Thomas Wolfe Embraces Life," *Catholic World*, CXLIII (April 1936), 42-48.

McCoy, George. "Asheville and Thomas Wolfe," *North Carolina Historical Review*, XXX (April 1953), 200-17.

McElderry, B. R., Jr. "The Autobiographical Problem in Thomas Wolfe's Earlier Novels," *Arizona Quarterly*, IV (Winter 1948), 315-24.

McGovern, Hugh. "A Note on Thomas Wolfe," *New Mexico Quarterly Review*, XVII (Summer 1947), 138-44.

Maclachlan, J. M. "Folk Concepts in the Novels of Thomas Wolfe," *Southern Folklore Quarterly*, IX (December 1945), 175-86.

Magus, Peter. "Thomas Wolfe," *Syn og Segn* [Oslo], LIII (March 1947), 138-44.

Meyerhoff, H. "Death of Genius: The Last Days of Thomas Wolfe," *Commentary*, XIII (January 1952), 44-51.

Middlebrook, Leah R. "Reminiscences of Thomas Wolfe," *American Mercury*, LXIII (November 1946), 544-49.

————. "Further Memories of Thomas Wolfe," *American Mercury*, LXIV (April 1947), 413-20.

Miller, Henry. "Mother and Son," *The Nation*, CLVI (June 5, 1943), 811.

Norman, James. "The Gargantuan Gusto of Thomas Wolfe," *Scholastic*, XXVII (November 2, 1935), 5.

Norwood, Hayden. "Julia Wolfe: Web of Memory," *Virginia Quarterly Review*, XX (April 1944), 236-50.

Perkins, Maxwell. "Thomas Wolfe," *Harvard Library Bulletin*, I (Autumn 1947), 269-77.

Powell, Desmond. "Of Thomas Wolfe," *Arizona Quarterly Review*, I (Spring 1945), 28-36.

Pugh, C. E. "Of Thomas Wolfe," *Mark Twain Quarterly*, VII (Summer-Fall 1945), 13-14.

Pusey, William W., III. "The German Vogue of Thomas Wolfe," *The Germanic Review*, April 1948, pp. 131-48.

Rascoe, Burton. "Of Time and Thomas Wolfe," *Newsweek*, July 26, 1939, p. 36.

———. "Wolfe, Farrell, and Hemingway," *American Mercury*, LI (December 1940), 493-94.

Robinson, H. M. "Thomas Wolfe as Writer and Man," *The Saturday Review of Literature*, XXXI (February 7, 1948), 8.

Schoenberner, Franz. "Wolfe's Genius Seen Afresh," *The New York Times Book Review*, August 4, 1946, 1. [Also in *The Inside Story of an Outsider* (New York, The Macmillan Company, 1949), and *The Enigma of Thomas Wolfe*, pp. 290-97.]

Simpson, C. M., Jr. "A Note on Thomas Wolfe," *Fantasy*, VI, No. 2 (1939), 17-21.

———. "Thomas Wolfe: A Chapter in His Biography," *Southwest Review*, XXV (April 1940), 308-21.

Slay, J. M. "Wolfe and Perkins," *The Saturday Review of Literature*, XXXIV (September 1, 1951), 27.

Smith, Harrison. "Midwife to Literature: Maxwell Perkins," *The Saturday Review of Literature*, XXX (July 12, 1947), 15-16.

Solon, S. L. "The Ordeal of Thomas Wolfe," *Modern Quarterly*, XI (Winter 1939), 45-53.

Spitz, Leon. "Was Wolfe an Anti-Semite?" *American Hebrew*, CLVIII (November 19, 1948), 5.

Stearns, M. M. "The Metaphysics of Thomas Wolfe," *College English*, VI (January 1945), 193-99. [Also in *The Enigma of Thomas Wolfe*, pp. 195-205.]

BIBLIOGRAPHY

Stokely, James. "Perkins and Wolfe," *The Saturday Review of Literature*, XXXIV (July 7, 1951), 22.

Stone, Geoffrey. "In Praise of Fury," *Commonweal*, XXII (May 10, 1935), 36-37.

Thompson, Betty. "Thomas Wolfe: Two Decades of Criticism," *South Atlantic Quarterly*, XLIX (July 1950), 378-92. [Also in *The Enigma of Thomas Wolfe*, pp. 298-313.]

Thompson, Lawrance. "Tom Wolfe, Amerikas Skildare," *Bonniers Litterära Magasin*, VIII (September 1939), 541-46.

Terry, John Skally. See Aswell (above).

Tibbell, John. "The Long Dream of Thomas Wolfe," *American Mercury*, LIII (December 1941), 752-54.

Todd, J. W. "Thomas Wolfe: Inexhaustible," *Scholastic*, XXXVIII (May 12, 1941), 23.

Volkening, H. T. "Tom Wolfe: Penance No More," *Virginia Quarterly Review*, V (Spring 1939), 196-215. [Also in *The Enigma of Thomas Wolfe*, pp. 33-50.]

Wade, J. D. "Prodigal," *Southern Review*, I (July 1935), 192-98.

Walser, Richard. "Some Notes on Wolfe's Reputation Abroad," *Carolina Quarterly*, I (March 1949), 37-48.

Warren, R. P. "The Hamlet of Thomas Wolfe," *The American Review*, V (September 1935), 191-208. [Also in *The Enigma of Thomas Wolfe*, pp. 120-32.]

Watkins, F. C. "Thomas Wolfe and the Southern Mountaineer," *South Atlantic Quarterly*, L (January 1951), 58-71.

Wolfe, Thomas. "The Story of a Novel," *The Saturday Review of Literature*, XII (December 14, 1935), 3-4, 12, 14, 16; (December 21, 1935), 3-4, 15; and (December 28, 1935), 3-4, 14-16.

————. "What a Writer Reads," *Book Buyer*, I (December 1935), 13-14.

―――. "Writing Is My Life," *The Atlantic*, CLXXVIII (December 1946), 60-66; CLXXIX (January 1947), 39-45 and (February 1947), 55-61.

―――. "Portrait of a Player," *Theatre Annual*, VI (1947), 43-54.

―――. "Something of My Life," *The Saturday Review of Literature*, XXXI (February 7, 1948), 6-8. [Also in *The Enigma of Thomas Wolfe*, pp. 3-7.]

―――. "You Can't Escape Autobiography," ed. R. D. Meade, *The Atlantic*, CLXXXVI (November 1950), 80-83.

Anon. "Wolfe in the West," *Newsweek,* July 2, 1950, p. 80.